Instagram Influencer Marketing Secrets 2019

Social Media Guide to Building Your Personal Brand; Proven Business Strategy to Become an Instagram Influencer and Make Money Online From Home

© **Copyright 2019 - All rights reserved.**

The content contained within this book may not be reproduced, duplicated or transmitted in any form or by any means without direct written permission from the author or the publisher.

Under no circumstances will any blame or legal responsibility be held against the publisher, or author, for any damages, reparation, or monetary loss due to the information contained within this book. Either directly or indirectly.

Legal Notice:

This book is copyright protected. You cannot amend, distribute, sell, use, quote or paraphrase any part, or the content within this book, without the consent of the author or publisher.

Disclaimer Notice:

The information contained within this document is for educational and entertainment purposes only. The information in this book is true and complete. However, no warranties of any kind are declared or implied. Readers acknowledge that the author/publisher is not engaging in the rendering of legal, financial, medical or professional advice. Please consult a licensed professional before attempting any techniques outlined in this book. By reading this document, the reader agrees that under no circumstances is the author responsible for any losses, direct or indirect, which are incurred as a result of the use of information contained within this document, including, but not limited to, — errors, omissions, or inaccuracies.

- Passion First 10
- Jazz Your Profile Up With A Memorable Bio 11
- Engage Your Audience Through Your Feed 12
- Continually Create Quality Content 14
- Focus on Engagement 16
- Post Content Consistently 19
- Use Instagram Stories Wisely 20
- Collaborate-Network 21
- Reach Out to Brands 21
- Zero Shortcuts 23

How To Get Paid By Big Brands And Partnerships 24
- Digital Products 24
- Brand Ambassadors 26
- Social Media Sponsored Posts 27
- Physical Products 28
- Affiliate Marketing 29
- Photography, Copywriting, and Creative Direction 32
- Events 32

Deciding Your Price as an Influencer 33
FINDING THE RIGHT BRAND TO WORK WITH 35

How to Research an Instagram Target Audience 37
- The Quickest Way To Research Your Instagram Audience 38
- Start with bigger marketing personas 38
- Check your Instagram demographics 40
- Stalk your followers 41

    A little DM never hurt anybody 44

    Check your competitions posts.. 44

    Ask directly in the feed 46

    Use Instagram Polls 46

    Use hashtags to discover your Instagram target audience.............. 48

    Check out the winning formula and continuously replicate it 49

    Post at the right time 50

Making Money on Instagram through Brand Collaboration And Sponsorships.. 52

    Which Influencers Attract Instagram Sponsorships........................ 53

        Micro-influencers 53

        Hyper-influencers... 54

        Macro Influencers 55

    How Do I Get Brand Sponsorship as an Instagram Influencer.......... 55

    What Brands Want From You In Exchange For Their Money (Sponsorships)... 58

Comprehensive Guide to Creating an Excellent Influencer Marketing Strategy... 60

    How to Create an Influencer Marketing Strategy 62

        Set Your Goals 62

        Picking A Preferred Type of Influencer Marketing Campaign...... 63

        Identify and Define Your Audience 65

        Find the Right Influencers 66

        Find Influencers using Backlinks... 67

        Find Influencers by Topics 68

        Qualify Your Influencers 69

        Designing the Campaign 76

        Creating Content Together 79

Executing the Campaign 80

Measuring Effectiveness 81

The Future of Influencer Marketing 85

Influencer Marketing Research Tools 86

Joining The Influencer Community: Best Platforms For Any Influencer
.... 89

Upfluence 89

Revfluence 90

FameBit 91

Traackr 92

IZEA 93

Julius 94

Klear 95

Mustr 96

Onalytica 97

Webfluential 98

MARKETING YOURSELF AS AN INTROVERTED INFLUENCER 99

What Do These Personalities Translate To Online 99

How To Succeed As An Introverted Influencer 100

Create A Routine 101

Engage at Your Highest 102

Challenge Yourself 102

Reciprocating Energy 102

Effective ways to market yourself as an introverted influencer: 103

Promoting Your Brand As An Introvert 105

Shy vs. Introvert 105

Finding the Right Strategy 107

Understanding Yourself 108

Selling Your Brand Without Selling 109

Relation and Education 109

Allow The Audience To Express Themselves 110

Sense of Humor Is Vital 111

Use the 80/20 Rule 111

Salesman Era Is Over 112

HOW BRANDS AND INFLUENCERS CAN MAKE MONEY TOGETHER 113

1. Networking 114

2. Content Sharing 115

4.   Partnerships 115

5.   Free Product Samples 116

1. National Geographic 118

2. Adidas Neo 119

3. Bloom & Wild 120

4. Bejeweled 120

5. Old Spice Dream Runner 121

6. Chanel 123

7. Sonic Drive-In 125

8. Airbnb 126

9. Hartley's 10 Cal Jelly 127

Creating The Best Instagram Captions As an Instagram Influencer ... 129

The Best Time to Post on Instagram 139

When are your followers online on Instagram? 141

Where to track your Instagram followers online 141

When are my Instagram followers online? 142

6

Experiment with posting times 142
What does Instagram analytics tell you? 142
Best time to post on Instagram 143
Choosing a schedule for posting content 144
Learning How to Increase Online Sales Exponentially in 2019 146
   The Best Ways to Increase Online Sales Fast 147
      Reap Trust 148
      Incorporate product videos 149
      Focus on your target audience 150
      Deploy live chat 152
      Improve your website's user experience 153
      Remove friction-creating elements on checkout pages 154
      Offer a guarantee 155
      Nurture your email list with unique content 157
      Try Crazy Egg Testing Tools to Increase Your Online Sales 158
      Respond to your followers on all channels 159
   Conclusion 160
21 Facts About Successful Online Businesses That Was Kept A Secret 161
   1. They grow fast 161
   2. They focus on the big picture 162
   3. They differentiate themselves 162
   4. They know when to give up 162
   5. They understand the value of great content 162
   6. Social media is their weapon 162
   7. They go all in 163
   8. They listen to their customers 163

9. They grow their list from day one 163

10. They pursue their passion 163

11. They know the value they produce, and they charge appropriately 164

12. They invest heavily in SEO 164

13. They solve a real problem 164

14. They take action before everything's perfect 164

15. They know that passive income is not passive 165

16. They stop looking for the golden goose 165

17. They outsource. Sometimes, A LOT 165

18. They have an actual plan (a written one) 165

19. They don't let failure beat them up 166

20. They utilize excellent tools to save time and money 166

21. They're dominating their niche 166

Influencer Marketing: Best Trends from 2018 And What To Look Forward To In 2019 167

It's harder than ever to get seen 167

Instagram Stories are a hot commodity 167

Engagement rates are the real metric 168

Agencies can pinch-hit when scale is needed 168

My Predictions 168

Brands need more transparency from influencers 168

Facebook Live is the new standard for Quality, Value, and Confidence 169

Agencies will provide influencer education as a service 169

The Final Word 170

Top 10 Nuggets to keep in mind 171

8

Instagram INFLUENCERS

Source: Fiverr.com

Instagram is an amazing and powerful tribune that carries huge value for brands, and with over 800 million monthly users, many brands have resorted to using it to target customers. Instagram users make purchases based on the recommendations of influencers. Various brands are seeing big returns from brand ambassador marketing and influencers rather than the traditional generic advertising.

According to influencer Central, Instagram influencers are the sixth when it comes to influencing consumer behavior.

These statistics have increased the number of people attempting to be Instagram influencers to different degrees of success. The million dollar question is how does one become an influencer? The simple answer is to emulate the tested recipes of success from successful Instagram Influencers. This guide will give an in-depth explanation of the steps you must take to be a successful Instagram Influencer.

Passion First

The first order of business as an influencer is to find something you're passionate about. This means doing the thing you love, so you should start with your hobbies and likes. You do not have to be an Instagram expert when you start, all you need is working knowledge of the practice and of course open to learning on the job.

Another important thing is to choose a niche that suits your personality. It is essential because you might not be successful in fields that others are successful at. The things that worked for others might not work for you no matter how hard you try. Therefore you should consider your options before starting your journey as an influencer on IG.

You'd be surprised to realize that your various hobbies like the pictures of your food, taking funny pictures with your dog, scenic views of different places, can funny captions can transform into a source of revenue if utilized. It is very important to be specific, not general.

For example, while most accounts are promoting different types of fitness, the well-paid and most popular ones stick to a particular niche subset of fitness such as keto diets or yoga.

Another important advice is not to follow different trends but things you're interested in and passionate about. A notable example is Karina Garcia, an Instagram influencer that successfully turned her interest in Slime into a 2 million dollars per year.

Jazz Your Profile Up With A Memorable Bio

After you have decided your niche, the next step is to fine-tune your IG account to fit the taste of your target market. The first thing to do is to create an impressive bio that grabs, and most importantly, keeps the attention of even a regular viewer.

The bio on Instagram is equivalent to a first impression, and it could make your Instagram swim or sink decent on how good it is. Your bio should be able to tell your story in a unique way that people can relate and connect to, and it should also be unique in some ways so you can stand out from others in your field.

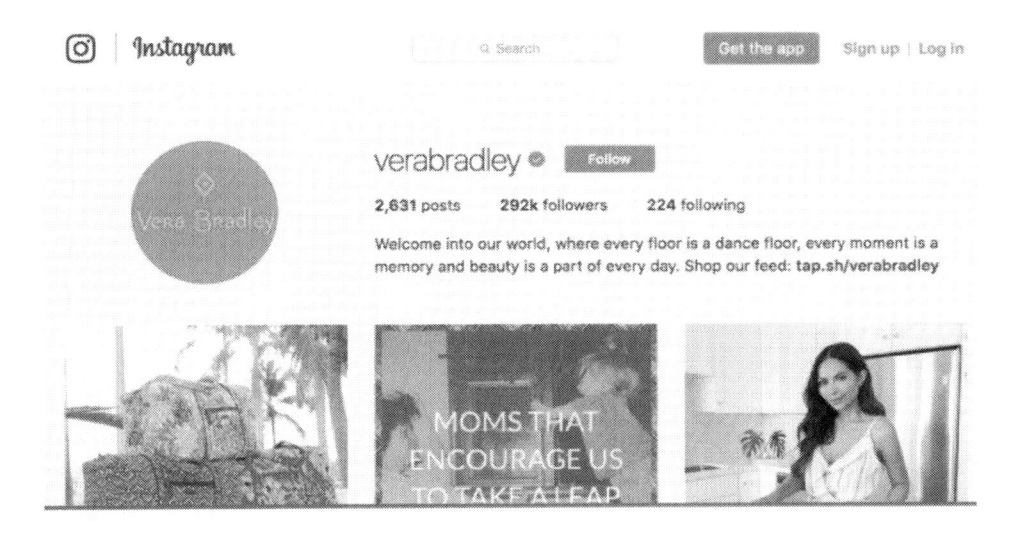

This can take different approaches, a bio that defines you and your brand or a short story that describes your journey. Also, you should try to avoid a bio that makes your page look like a CV or resume.

It is imperative to consider searches when developing your bio. Vera Bradley is a notable example of an influencer who has an attractive and compelling Instagram bio. In the name field, she purposely included "dance" to make her profile show up every time the phrase is searched.

Engage Your Audience Through Your Feed

One of the most critical things that set an influencer account apart from a regular account is having a consistent aesthetic. Every one of your photos should not just be visually appealing, they should also adhere to an overall theme.

A well-planned and cohesive outfeed helps both dedicated and casual viewers to know what to expect from your account with a quick swipe through your feed.

It also helps to increase engagement on your profile by keeping people on your feed longer since they'll feel compelled to like other pictures as they scroll down to your feed to see how great your taste is, and how the images fit with the rest of the page.

This means it is essential for you to decide the type of aesthetic you want your IG page to show so you can stick to it.

Most IG influencers employ a unique style of editing their photos and videos, so the composition and color is uniform. Tools like Lightroom and VSCO are handy for editing photos since they have more filters than the generic one on Instagram.

Continually Create Quality Content

This is where your efforts will be decided. Packaging is important, but it is more crucial that the quality of the product that's being packaged to be as flawless as possible. Make sure you create your best content.

Since it is your brand, you should make it a reflection of your vision, rather than a copy of another. Also, don't be scared to invest your money when need be. Your brand is your business, so don't be afraid to spend on equipment that will improve the quality of your content. It is essential to create quality contents consistently, and they should be relevant to your target audience if you ever want to be a top influencer.

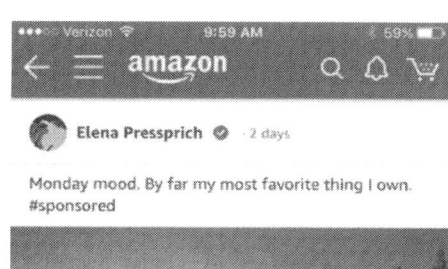

The quality of the content you post will determine whether people will follow your account and engage with your content or not. Low-quality pictures will not attract followers but if you share high-quality images that educate, entertain, or attract people?

The casual viewers and followers will come in packs in response to the contents that captivates them.

Making great content is an Instagram influencers job, no matter the form of the content. Identify what your audience desires and give it to them. If you want to your paid for Instagram posts, you have to prove that you're worth it to the market by creating new contents that help solve problems for your niche audience in an exciting way.

If you want to grow your account, you need to invest in decent equipment such as a DSLR camera or a smartphone and also spend some time taking photos that have a good lighting, solid composition, and have focus in all the right places. You should also make sure your captions are good enough to encourage engagement.

Focus on Engagement

Most of the successful Instagram influencers do not just post contents and leave it there. Instead, they usually put a question by the caption, and they reply to the DMS, comments, and engaging with other accounts.

This will create a relationship between you and your followers around the brand, and turn usual swipers into super fans.

When brands research the influencers to partner with, nothing is worse than an account with "empty" followers. This is the usual result why there are a lot of followers, but there is little to no engagement on the content. Pages with "empty" followers usually look manufactured and unrealistic, and since the target of most brands is actual active users, lack of engagement objects your page will reduce your chances of securing brands to work with.

Therefore, it is very crucial that you create content that encourages engagement. This can be done through the use of products as the captions to your posts or the use of stories about your life. You can improve the engagement of your post by replying comments in a way that makes your audience feel like they have something in common with you.

A good relationship between your followers are you is important because if your content is excellent and a connection exists, your followers and fans will hopefully share your content on your behalf. In other words, great content motivated by engagement amplifies audience engagement(likes, comments, shares) effortlessly. FashioNova does this excellently from time to time

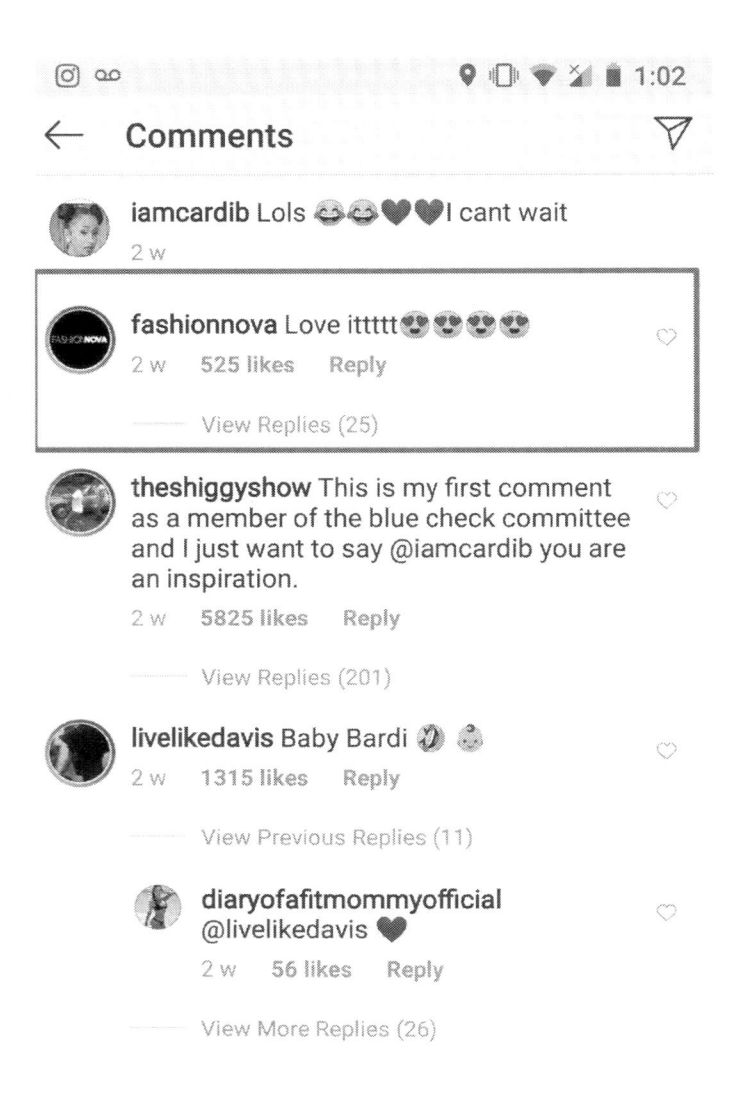

> **Comments**
>
> **iamcardib** Lols 😂😂🖤🖤 I cant wait
> 2 w
>
> **fashionnova** Love ittttt 😍😍😍😍
> 2 w   525 likes   Reply
> ──── View Replies (25)
>
> **theshiggyshow** This is my first comment as a member of the blue check committee and I just want to say @iamcardib you are an inspiration.
> 2 w   5825 likes   Reply
> ──── View Replies (201)
>
> **livelikedavis** Baby Bardi 🍼👶
> 2 w   1315 likes   Reply
> ──── View Previous Replies (11)
>
> **diaryofafitmommyofficial** @livelikedavis 🖤
> 2 w   56 likes   Reply
> ──── View More Replies (26)

In addition to producing quality content that improves engagement, you can also invite targeted traffic to your website by taking the following steps:

- Look for guests blogging opportunities to amplify your content outreach
- Offer your contents to blogs in your field that offer annual content roundups. These folks are hungry for good content are on the hunt for the next amazing thing to

curate. If your content measures up to their criteria, it will be on their website, and you will reap all the traffic and visibility rewards
- Connect all your social media accounts, so your content can be pushed on simultaneously
- Add a call-to-action in your caption
- Link all your social media accounts to ensure your content is pushed on all simultaneously
- Include a call-to-action in your caption
- Post during the day when you'd be likely to get the best engagement. Insights can also help you find the best times if you have a business account.
- Host contests and giveaways
- Follow comparable accounts and engage with their content

You should note that the more the targeted traffic you receive, the higher your content engagement rate. Requesting feedback from your followers is also a fantastic way to understand what makes them tick (which helps to figure out where to drive your content) while strengthening the relationship between them and your brand.

Post Content Consistently

Another essential requirement for an Instagram influencer is to post consistently. Instagram's algorithm helps to reward consistency. This is because Instagram gains revenue through consistent use, accounts that help Instagram achieve that get pushed up higher in the newsfeed. Your audience also requires you to be regular, so they know, without having to think hard about it, when contents are available.

You can use tools like Preview, Planoly, and Later to plan out York feed for the week. You can easily take an hour of your day to make content for the week, so you don't miss deadlines, and your content gets posted regardless of personal or network issues.

Planoly and Preview are both free to use, but try the latter allows only 30 photos per month on an Instagram account. Buffer allows you to schedule 10 posts for free for any three social media accounts. Ripley is available at $9.99 per month.

Use Instagram Stories Wisely

With the introduction of Instagram stories, many users have taken to using it to give their followers and insight into their lives. It is now one of the most excellent tools to increase visibility and grow more followers.

Another beautiful part about Instagram stories is that people that aren't your followers can discover your account from your Stories. Adding hashtags, locations, and other little details that narrow search terms to Stories, you can be quickly discovered by more people outside your niche. If you have over 10,000 followers, another benefit is that you can easily include an outbound link with the "swipe up" option on stories.

Another way to utilize the "Stories" option is by giving shout-outs and tagging other accounts. This serves the purpose of building relationships while growing your following.

Collaborate-Network

It is possible for you to grow and account by yourself, but collaborating with other is the easiest and fastest ways to increase your audience. However, you should know that working with a bigger influencer will be advantageous at your end than theirs because there is more in it for you than there is for the significant influencer.

This will also allow you to network on your niche and bring you closer to opportunities that you are not familiar with initially. You can also do this by going through favorites hashtags and seeing similar accounts. Engage with contents, start a conversation, and you might end up collaborating and meeting in real life.

Reach Out to Brands

After you have defined your audience and brand and have started creating quality content, you will start getting a picture of the type of business you will profit from a partnership with you. Start small, for example, if you're interested in clothing, don't go straight for GUCCI.

Instead, start by tagging small clothes start-ups that match the identity of your brand when you wear their product. Even if you're not getting paid to advertise or wear their products, doing this will put you on their radar as an ambassador for their brand. \

Different brands, both outside and in your niche, want to work with influencers in social media and have agencies or teams with the primary purpose of finding the right people to contact. Optics like engagement rates and follower count matter and because it is all so new, it is the first thing most brands take notice of. They want to see lots of quality content and followers, preferably all content that matches their brand ideals.

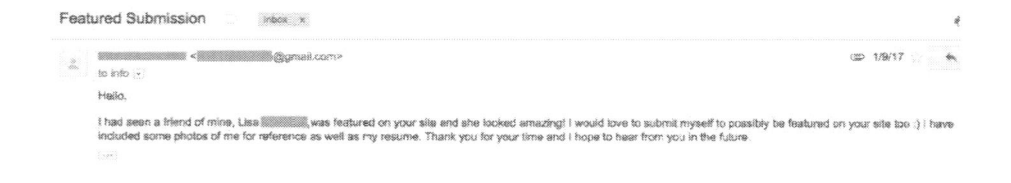

After you have grown your account to a suitable benchmark, which is usually at least 1,000 followers, it's time to start reaching out to brands in your niche. After you have followed the above steps, you have a better chance of landing branding opportunities.

You need to spend time practicing, detailing, and crafting your pitch while also preparing for possible questions. Pitching takes some experience to master, so you need to be mentally prepared to learn and to fail sometimes.

Zero Shortcuts

Everything up until now has been quite simple, but if you want to stand out and succeed at being an Influencer, you're going to above and beyond your peers to see good results. You can achieve this by turning your hobby into a paying job by developing a passionate, unstoppable attitude.

You must have the willingness to churn out great content consistently while possessing the patience needed for the months it will take to build a noticeable online presence. This is the only way to rule your particular field and raise your profile above the competition.

This is why it is crucial to start with a system in place that allows you freedom and room to create while not restricting you. You can also organize different ideas and categorize in various categories like ideas that will work, those that might work, and those that won't. Creating a system that works is very important.

It is also crucial to know your audience well. Start by gathering some basics like age, gender, geographical location of your main demographic. Find out the post that is most liked and the time of year when you get most of your engagement. Using all these data is key to your growth as an influencer and is to use in convincing different brands to work with you.

This information will also help you to find the particular brand that will be successful from using you as a sponsor. Most brands want to hit a specific market when they collaborate with you. If you swing to a business account, you can quickly dig up data in your Instagram Analytics report. This will give you an edge when it's time to negotiate.

Another important advice that usually gets overlooked by people to be an influencer is this**: DO NOT BUY FOLLOWERS**. There are agencies and tool brands dedicated to sniffing out cheaters. Being a prospective brand influencer is not something that can be faked. Even though this is a new market, it is evolving continuously, and it is becoming impossible to cheat the system.

How To Get Paid By Big Brands And Partnerships

Influencer marketing has exploded recently because most leading brands know that social media influencers drive awareness more than others. But how do influencers make money?

"Influencing" is a full-time job for influencers and is often made up of few roles likes community engagement, design, public speaking, photography, content creation, and more.
We will explore several ways for influencers to leverage their expertise, skills, and influence to make money from various revenue streams by supporting brands in digital marketing.

Digital Products

E-products are now increasingly popular for influencers to make money because the products are relatively easy to produce and cheap. Another added benefit is their ability to scale rapidly online with seamless distribution. Digital products can vary anywhere from a downloadable travel guide, e-book or workout program, to an organizational template or one-page meal.

E-products have given influencers the opportunity to create tangible things that they can sell and distribute to their network to earn an income for their influence, expertise, and knowledge. A simple example is the Raven Loso, who was able to convert the popularity she gained through the posting of her pictures into creating an apparel line with over 2 million followers.

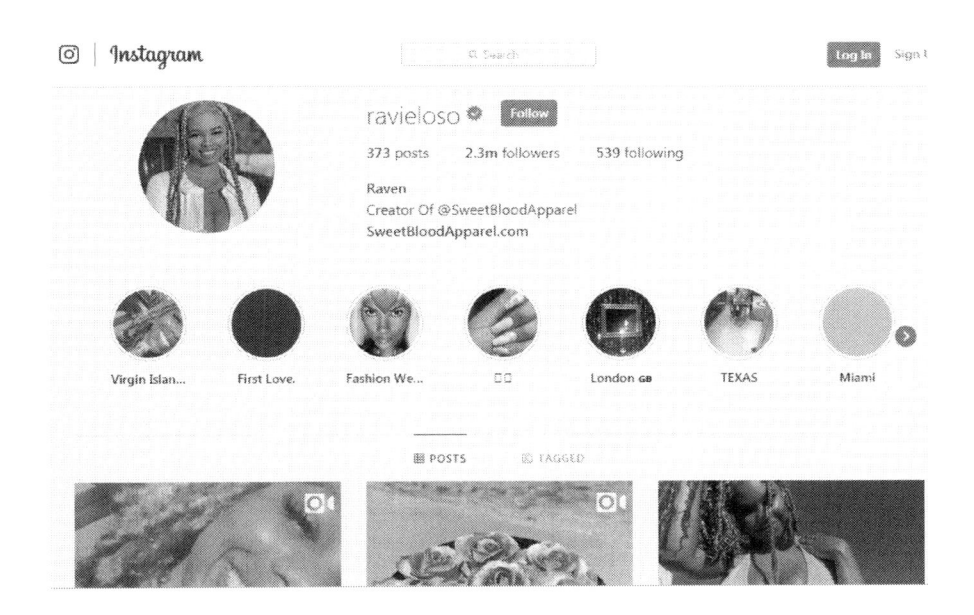

Another important way influencers make money from digital products in collaboration with brands to create products by selling editorial and advertising space to them or by being commissioned to create content. Example are authors like The Oatmeal who used their platforms to promote and create their self-centered e-books.

Brand Ambassadors

Another way to make money as a new influencer is to become a brand ambassador. This is currently known as the best method of influencers marketing. Companies now hire brand ambassadors for long-term roles and pay then on a basis. If you chose that path, it is your responsibility to become the supreme expert on the product or brand and ensure that your partnership with the brand on every social media channel.

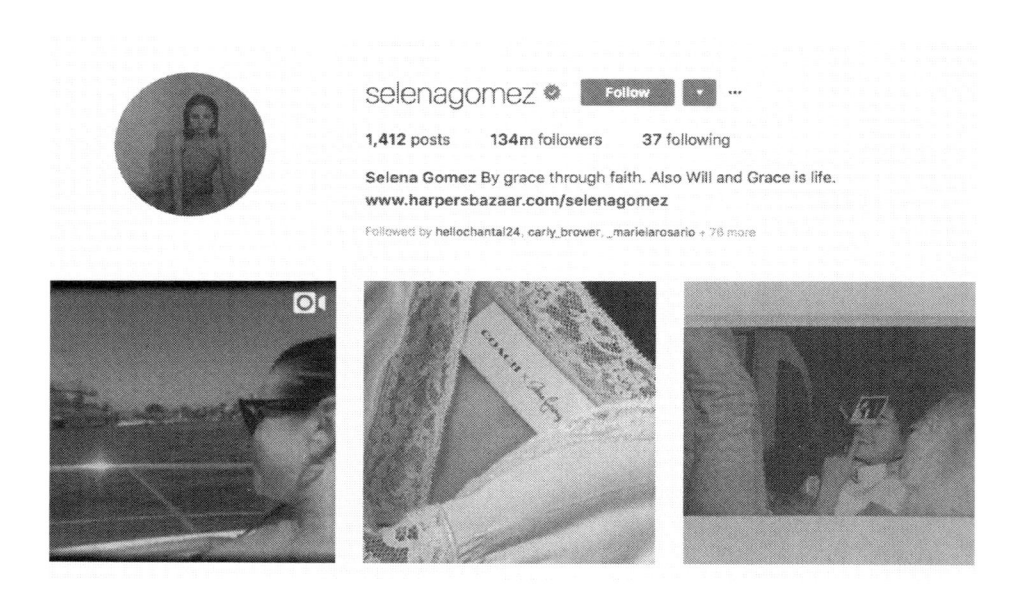

Brands usually employ ambassadors they consider to be a great fit for their target market and brand. Most of the time, brand ambassadors are usually celebrities and big-time influencers, they can also be micro-influencers, depending on the goals of the brand and the campaign.

Selena Gomez is the undisputed queen of Instagram with 128 million followers which has seen the likes of Coach partner with her to sell their brand.

Social Media Sponsored Posts

As an influencer, you should propose to brands to help them promote their products on your posts. Influencers have the power to convince audiences about trends due to the level of trust they got due to their online presence.

Brand ambassador relationships are usually long-term partnerships, and sponsored social media are used as an approach to creating brand exposure and awareness. This is one of the ways influencers make money, especially for influencers that are starting with few followers.

A sponsored post is what happens when a brand uses an influencer to create a content featuring their brand to push it to their audience. There are many types of this, from wearing branded clothing, promoting a new product, developing unique imagery, sharing the brand owned content, generating exposure among a new target market and launching a new brand.

Some brands often reach out to good influencers for collaborations, and it is also important to find brands that match your niche which ensuring the brands appeal to your audience. You can also look for brands directly (through their website or Instagram) to negotiate a deal, and you can also list yourself on an influencer platform to improve your chances of being found by a big fish.

Beware of disclosure guidelines and regulations when you're exchanging money and other payment forms with a brand in some territories and countries. In certain climes, you have to include links and show that it is a sponsored post in the terms and condition page on the brand's page.

Another vital piece of advice, don't lose the trust your audience has in you just because you're looking to make a quick buck via sponsored posts. This is why it is essential to indicate if it's a sponsored post with a hashtag (for example, by adding #sponsored)

Physical Products

A new way to create revenue in conjunction with a brand is to create a physical product, range or collection together. This type of influencer monetization is seen across various niche from co-branded brute products and fashion capsule collections to fitness, travel, food, and health products.

You can purchase products from suppliers to see lots or sell the products you produce yourself. While considered as a conventional way of e-retailing, it involves stocking some inventory, which means you'd need some startup capital to buy the products and storage space for the products. It also includes sorting the delivery costs and logistics.

Influencers get money by co-creating contents and receiving an amount of commission on all sales, or a particular fee for the partnership (same as an ambassador program), depending on the agreement made. A commission-based model also improves sales for an influencer because it allows ten to maximize their income especially if the product is successful, and they don't need any cost upfront.

An excellent example of this is "Slime Queen Karina," she built an empire outside her YouTube channel and Instagram by selling materials in conjunction with 'Target.' With this, she can bring revenue to both Target and herself.

By marketing your products, you don't have to worry about messages from other brands in your posting strategy. Instead, you can focus all your creative energy on pushing your brand on the commodities you sell.

Affiliate Marketing

Affiliate marketing is comparable to commission-based arrangements in that sales can be attributed to their content or post, and the referral partner receives part of the sale. The difference between an affiliate and an influencer is that an affiliate works towards making sales for or a partnering brand in exchange for a commission.

There are some outlets that you can work within the affiliate marketing network namely:
- **Stylinity:** It is ideal for accounts that are in the fashion niche. With this site, anyone shopping through your link means you receive a sizeable commission for helping the company advertise the particular product.
- **Sharesale:** Is a platform that helps you choose from a list of businesses that you would love to help advertise for, you can enroll in their program, but the site checks your engagement reach before they partner with you which is

why it is important to take the first two steps I highlighted seriously.

- **Ebates:** Is discount dealership of sorts. It requires you to promote deals and discounts for interested parties. With each click of the link, you receive a commission.

With the above three, you can insert the URL link or shorten and customize it using the [bitly website]().

This type of marketing is easy, and you get to do what you love. These companies even provide outfits or tech that you use to make these ads and that is an added plus no doubt. Below is an example of Kristyn from @Glamourzine who epitomes the perfect description of affiliate marketing.

Apart from owning and rocking those boots provided by the company, Kristyn gets to receive a commission on every click on the link. What more could she ask for? You too can be like Kristyn by following the steps enumerated above.

While the sole aim of an influencer is to create awareness, it's a good way to ensure influencers relieve income for their efforts and to track the success of influencer engagement. Affiliate marketing is usually on a pay-per-click, pay-per-sale, or a pay-per-lead model.

It's a great way for influencers to earn an income from the brands they naturally love, endorse, and support. It is also an excellent way for brands to measure how much influence an influencer has objectively.

Affiliate marketing is usually not the only source of income for influencers; since it is not reliable or steady, however, it is an excellent way to earn revenue. This is normally don't with the use of traceable referral codes that shows the particular referral partner that influence the sale.

It is crucial to create engaging posts, so you can promote different products without being pushy or trying too hard. This method might be challenging at first, but with time you will learn the art of pushing products in posts without coming across as preachy or pushy.

Instagram only allow links in your bio, so you have to focus on a product at a time which means you must rely on the promo code if you decide to focus on affiliate links, and it is advisable that influencers use it on a broader audience. While you can easily reach out to popular affiliate programs, you can also explore affiliate marketplaces like RewardStyle, Amazon, and ClickBank for more options.

Photography, Copywriting, and Creative Direction

Instagram is about visual contents. Therefore, in addition to monetizing their social networks and influence, an influencer can also choose to leverage their skills such as copywriting, strategic consulting, photography, creative direction, and such to make money.

While influencers are content creators, most importantly, they are also business-hungry creatures that used their skills to create a personal brand that provides revenue. So, brands usually work with influencers by hiring them as a freelancer.

However, you can sell your photos as prints and on other products like paintings, animations, videos, photos, and other video or image-based virtual products. On every post, refer your reader to visit the link in your bio. You can easily make your content accessible using the right hashtags to promote your photography portfolio.

Sites like Twenty20 and 500px serve as marketplaces where publishers and brands might license them while Teelaunch and Printful are tools that are useful for putting your photos on products.

Events

Influencers also make money sometimes by hosting store appearances or industry-related events. They leverage their following through the use of presentations to attract more presence to a new product or event.

A good example is the Canva event. Canva invited Australian beauty and fashion influencers like Sue Zimmerman and Kim Reynolds to host and attend the event. Influencers have great connections with their following, and they help to build hype around various events.

Deciding Your Price as an Influencer

Now that you are aware of the various ways to make money as an Instagram influencer with a plan in place, it is essential to figure out the worth of your contents. However, since the marketplace is quite obtuse, there is no clear answer to how much influencers get paid.

If you have influencer or brand ambassador friends, ask them how they get paid. Don't blindly accept an offer without determining what your real market value is. The current industry standard is $10 for 100 followers, it sometimes varies with the number of likes per posts, and as you grow, you should charge more.

It is mostly advisable to have a minimum set, but sometimes you should negotiate on a basis for special deals like putting their link in your bio or including the brand on your Instagram stories.

Most of these deals involve the creation of content and are usually negotiable. They can include an entire campaign or a single post in exchange for a fee, a service, a gift, a free product, the promise of exposure, and sometimes a combination.

You should know that when you're negotiating with a particular brand, you're not Just offering content, you're also increasing your followers and audience because these brands will use the content on their platforms, therefore, increasing the chances of converting the usual swipers into dedicated followers.

While money can be quite enticing, if you plan on being an Influencer on a long run, you should focus on making lasting relationships through experiences before creating rate sheets or raising your prices. This does not mean you should devalue your work. Instead, it is better to learn about the downsides and benefits of influencer marketing before asking for hefty prices.

FINDING THE RIGHT BRAND TO WORK WITH

If you're big enough, different brands will find you. You can also look for various brands to work with that are on the same level with you when it comes to personality and values, so your audience and followers won't feel like you're "selling out."

You can go to then directly to work out a deal, but you can otherwise list yourself on different influencer marketplaces out there to increase your chances.

- **Shoutcart:** Sell a "shout out" on behalf of a brand to your audience.

- **Fohr Card:** Link your blog, YouTube channel, Instagram, and various social platforms to create an "influencer card" that will show your various profiles and total reach for brands looking around for a partner. You can even get access to a list of various brands and what they want so that you can reach out to them easily.

- **Grapevine:** After you have gotten up to 5000 followers, you will be able to list yourself in the Grapevine market for the chance to work with similar-minded people.

- **Crowd Tap:** Use small content creation take to gain rewards. This is great for influencers with a small audience. Available in U.S.A only.

- **indaHash:** various brands can put up campaigns that you can participate in. You have to post a picture with a particular hashtag to get paid. You need only 700 followers to be eligible.

There are sets of predefined rules when it comes to sponsored post, don't forget to put the #sponsored hashtag on all sponsored post your audience trust. Almost 69% of influencers in a particular report said being transparent about their sponsorship did not affect the way consumers perceived their recommendation.

You should learn about how Instagrammers integrate brands in their stories and fudge different examples of sponsored posts by searching #sponsored on Instagram, below is an example of how "HowHeAsked" shared a sponsored post:

Today is a great day – it's a @ShaneCompany takeover day! We're sharing some of our most-loved designs throughout the day, so be free to chime in if you're into them too. The first does not need any introduction – we're always a fan of showstoppers ▢ More rings through the link in our profile!

Instagram also has a "Paid Partnership with" tag that mostly identifies sponsored posts, which some brands might need you to use to disclose the relationship between the both of you.

How to Research an Instagram Target Audience

Instagram audience should be on top of your list when it comes to developing an Instagram strategy. Think about it. If you want great contents, you have to know your followers' interests, and what's they'll like to see on their feeds.

Producing a killer content also requires you to know the voice that seems relatable to your audience.

To find the best time to post, you are required to know when your audience will be online.

Additionally, if you wish to experience the best of Instagram as a brand, you need to know about your target audience vividly. Actionable insights into your audience preferences, behavior, and interest will go a long way in the road to a successful Instagram strategy.

The most crucial question is, how can one find a target audience on Instagram? And where to look for it.

If you have the same series of questions on your mind too, here is some helpful information as found on the Iconosquare blog.

The Quickest Way To Research Your Instagram Audience

Start with bigger marketing personas

If you're a business person, you probably have a buyer personal already – the profile of an ideal target customer that you want your product to reach.

You need to reuse this information when you're defining your ideal Instagram audience – you don't need to reinvent the wheel. Ask your marketing team about the features of a typical customer. You should also dig into Instagram Analytics to be able to add more details and nuance to the customers' profile through your social media data.

You've got to ask yourself these four questions first:

- What is my product?
- What is my audience looking for?
- What audience do I want to attract? (Or, who is my product designed for?)
- And, what is the best way to attract that audience?

For example, let's look at @recreationalstudio, a Sydney-based jewelry account.

The brand sells pieces of jewelry. But they're more specific than that. They sell 9k gold pieces of jewelry, made in Italy, with a minimalist design, complete with price tag.

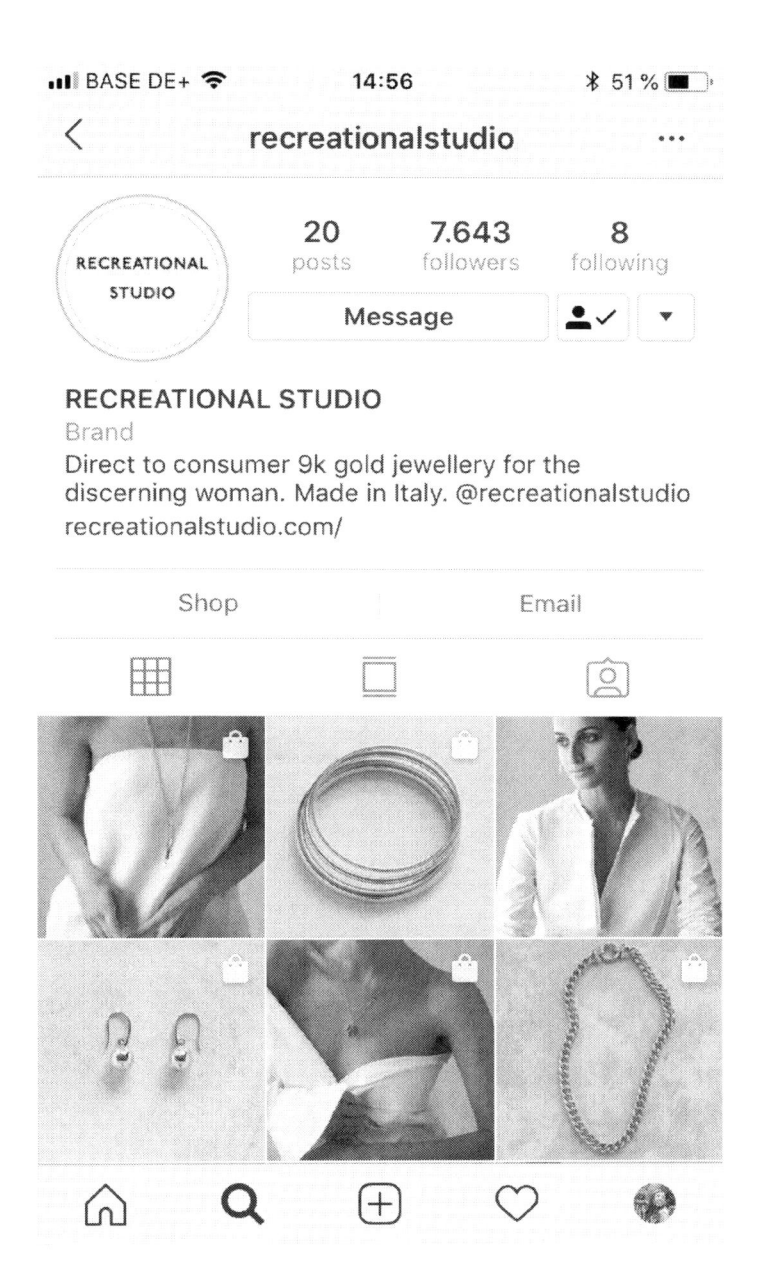

This means that their target audience must like gold, should have a taste for minimalist designs, should enjoy high-end products, and most importantly should be able to afford them.

This means there are some things to be thoroughly checked before considering an ideal customer, both online and offline.

For starters, you can easily rely on your existing buyer personal. However, you should know that there might be a significant difference between your usual target customers on Instagram and the ones that buy the products offline. This is why it is crucial to make sure your buyer persona is aligned with your demographic data from Instagram.

Check your Instagram demographics

At the beginning of your research, demographic insights on your Instagram audience can be beneficial. Look for Insights on your Instagram app and click the Audience. You'll be able to sit the most fundamental statistics of your followers such as they age, their gender, and their location.

This is also super important since you might want to run Instagram ads in the future since it'll help to get your content in front of your target audience through this data.

This will also help you to grow useful insights into the people that are following you. For example, if the target audience is predominantly middle-aged men, but Instagram tells you that most of your followers are millennial women, you should know something is wrong with your posting strategy, and you might want to rethink it.

But, if your buyer persona is generally in agreement with your demographic statistics on Instagram, then Kudos!

Now that you know this, the next important step is to understand what your audience is looking for.

Let us use the @recreationalstudio as an example again.

From the previous general research, we know their usual audience is obsessed with elegant, minimalist jewelry, with a blend of luxury. The trick here is to understand what the audience that wants this type of product is searching for on Instagram to be specific.

In other words, why are they on Instagram?

Or are they looking for jewelry tips?

Or want to educate themselves about different karat types?

Or perhaps they're interested in a behind-the-scenes look at how the jewelry is made?

Are they looking for inspiration on Instagram?

You can never get this type of information from demographic statistics merely because they're just demographic and not qualitative. The most critical role in audience research lies in finding your tarry followers interests, preferences, life philosophies, and habit – things that statistics can't show.

How do you find this out?

Follow the next steps in this guide.

Stalk your followers

This is definitely something you should never do in real life, but it is quite ideal when it comes to your Instagram target Audience research.

The best place to start is by engaging with the people that are already following you.

Go onto your Instagram.

Click on the people that commented or liked your latest posts. This will direct you to their accounts. For there, you can see what they're posting themselves, their hashtags, and most interestingly, the kind of captions they write and the language used. If your followers use abbreviations like YOLO AND LOL, or the use a lot of emojis, you should also consider using those elements on your captions too to make them more relatable.

When you've done that, you should also check your followers following to see who they interact with themselves.

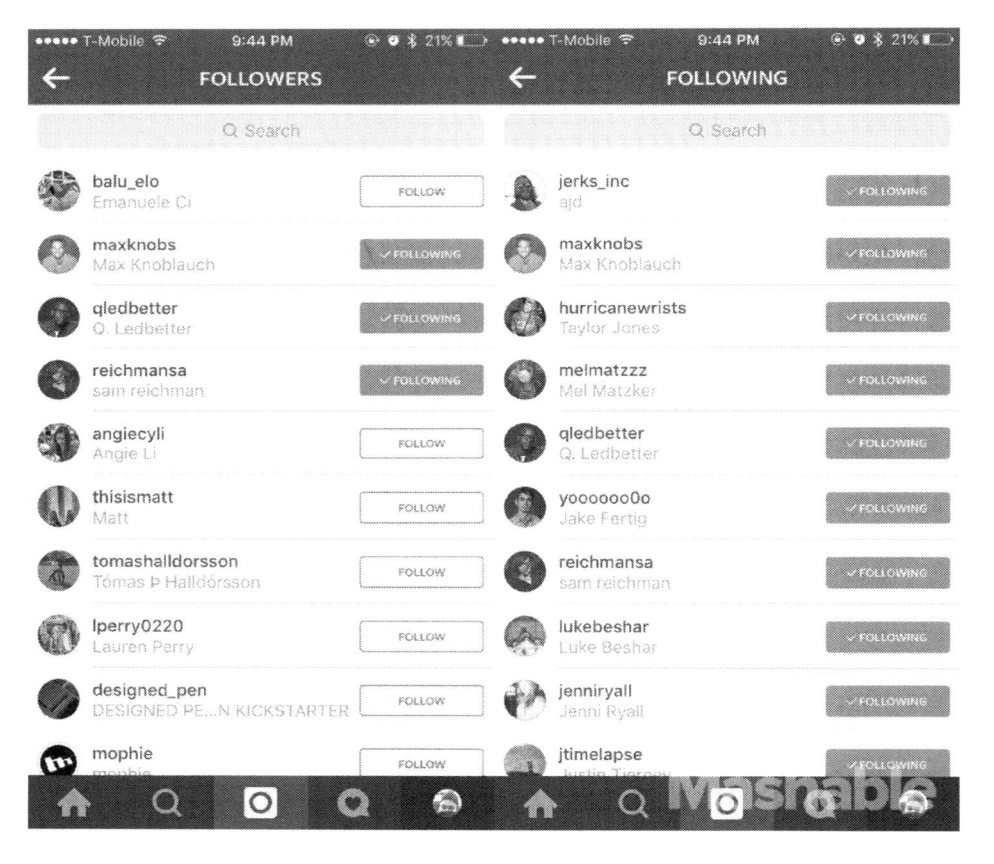

This process will give you an indication of what they are looking for on Instagram. The might be following some of your competitors and other accounts you're not aware of. You might also find various interests you didn't think they might have. For example, some of them might be architectural geeks apart from being your followers. They might also be interior design lovers that followers a lot of fashion influencers and some might follow the #scandinaviandesign.

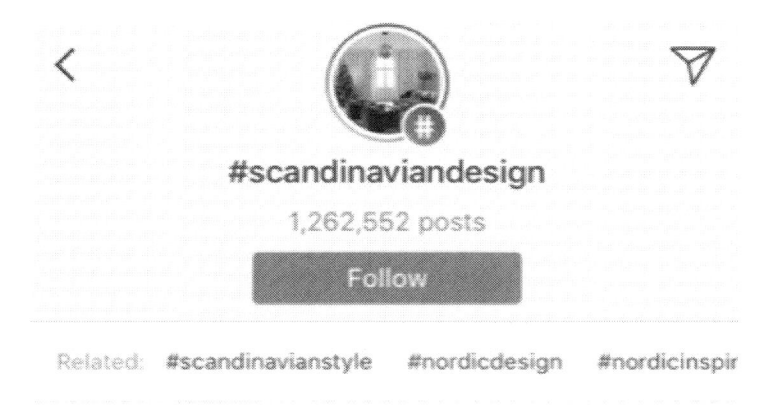

How can you use this information? Simple.

Let's take for example if your followers also followers' different types of inspirational quotes account. You can easily post an inspirational quote yourself in a while, and see the resonance you'll get with your audience. Here's another example, if you discovered that most of your followers follow one particular fashion influencer, you could reach out to create a co-marketing campaign together! You'll get the best results!

You get the idea.

A little DM never hurt anybody

It is quite okay to send a DM to your new follower asking why they've decided to follow you and what they'll expect to see on your account. Especially if you have noticed that they drop likes on your content regularly, or better if the comment on your posts all the time. So, don't wait time, slide in their DMs with a standard message!

Here's a sample:

Hi, we noticed you have been following us for a while, we appreciate you and your engagement! Quick Question: what is the kind of contents you'll like to see in our posts? We're trying to provide the best ABC to our followers, and your feedback is crucial to this, Cheers!

Easy peasy. Just be cool about it.

Check your competitions posts

Another simple way to find an ideal target audience is to steal from a competitor directly. Now, you are thinking I just might be crazy. But I can assure you that an effective way to find your ideal Instagram target audience is to steal one from your direct competitors.

I know it does not sound feasible but hear me out. First, know your competitors. Poplar analytics company, Iconosquare offer tools that can perform this task.

Then, check their profiles and take note of two things:

What's the engagement on their posts?

What do they post?

Let's say, for example, you're a German-Indian fair trade, with a clothing store account like @jrotifairworks. One of your indirect competitors would be @hemper_, a brand that sells homemade backpack through sustainable production in Nepal, with an audience that is into sustainable fashion. If you look into their account, you'll see that they often post Nepal travel content that helps them gain high engagement rates apart from their usual posting of product pics. The travel content is the ones that have the highest engagement rates in comparison to all other things on their field.

This means the followers of Hemper's are not following the brand because of the products they sell only – some flow the brand for community, inspiration, and the overall brand experience that lead to content diversity on the feed.

Therefore, as a German-Indian fair trade clothing account, posting some Indian-inspired content will help a lot. It might attract some followers and audiences that are "hanging around" at your competitors' accounts!

Also, you can also directly check the people that are commenting on and liking your competitors' pages - and like and comment back! If you consider yourself brave enough, you can do it directly on your competitors' page. Just make sure you're not being a pest and messing around. The idea is to feel relatable and engaging.

These tips will work like magic especially if you're starting from scratch and you're not with a lot of followers at the moment.

Ask directly in the feed

The power and importance of asking are quite undervalued in marketing. This is quite a bit, because, if you don't ask, you'll never know what your audience is into. Even Kim Kardashian isn't shy to ask for feedback from her followers. Last year, she asked her followers in her feed about the kind of aesthetic they into, this was because she was looking to develop a consistent theme on her Instagram.

End your captions with a simple question and ask your followers about what they'll like to see on your page. The kind of content? The type of format? Feed or Stories? Caption or No Caption?

Don't be afraid to ask!

Use Instagram Polls

You can also use Instagram polls to easily research team kind of content your audience would prefer to see in your feed. Of course, you'll have an idea of why you're being followed in the first place, but it won't hurt to ask again so you'll be sure you're on the right – or at least you'll be able to know I you're not.

National Geographic, with an audience that is travel-focused, uses their Stories polls once in a whole to know the kind of destination their followers like and finds more attractive, therefore, knowing the type of content that'll be more engaging for them.

If most people voted for "water" in the second poll, this might indicate that "waterfalls you should visit in 2019" will be quite engaging if published in the field. On the contrary, if the audience does not vote for 'Ice' at all, they're probably not interested in the topic, therefore, no matter how beautiful your post is, it won't be very engaging.

Use Instagram Polls for personal research. Ask various questions, as you did with the CTA's in your captions. Ask for the topics they're interested in and the formats they'll find more engaging. Do try like short videos? Carousels? You can even ask why they're following you in the first place.

Therefore, asking for valuable insights will help you refine your content strategy to make it more appealing to your target audience.

Use hashtags to discover your Instagram target audience

When it comes to Instagram, being the right hashtags can increase your reach dramatically on the platform. Using a hashtag puts you directly in front of the right audience.

However, most people use hashtags in an acquiescent manner, that is; they do little research, use them, and hope for the best.

A target hashtag is a form of a hashtag that your audience can use on their posts themselves. Therefore, the best thing is to be proactive. You should have the same interests as your target audience, so if you follow and use the same hashtags, it's a clear indication that you're a good match!

1. #LOVE
2. #INSTAGOOD
3. #PHOTOOFTHEDAY
4. #FASHION
5. #BEAUTIFUL
6. #HAPPY
7. #LIKE4LIKE
8. #PICOFTHEDAY
9. #ART
10. #PHOTOGRAPHY

Source: Metricool

Make sure you research well-targeted hashtags! Also, take an active approach and engage with the content on these hashtags. If you see something that's relevant to you, make sure you like it!

After that, go to the users profile and like their recent photos. It is okay to leave a few comments (make sure they're meaningful), and if you feel the user is a perfect audience, you are free to give them a follow.

It is normal to follow other people as a brand, especially if you're starting your Instagram journey. Just make sure you're not doing the shameless follow-for-follow and unfollowing instantly. Instead, try to make a meaningful connection with people that could be your potential perfect follower.

Check out the winning formula and continuously replicate it

If you've been posting for quite a while, you should start looking at the engagement rates of your posts to know the kind of contents your audience finds more interesting – and replicate those contents in the future to get more engagement. Your ideal Instagram audience are those that are interested in your content and are eager to interact – therefore, the goal is to look for a similar, lookalike audience by posting related content that was successful before.

For instance, when I checked Olga Rabo'saccount (Analytics → Engagement), I found out that her followers engage more in portrait photos. Also, they tend to interact more with carousels, than usual posts.

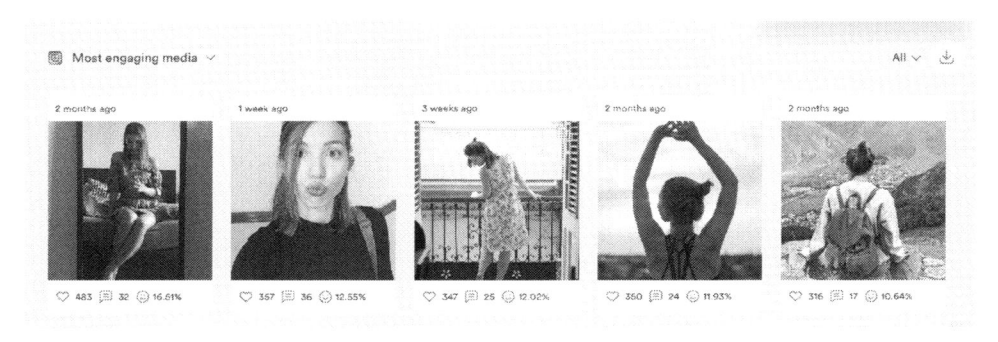

Therefore, if I want to gain more followers and attract more engagement through my post, I should probably post more carousels and more selfies.

Get what I mean?

Post at the right time

If you want to reach your Instagram target audience, you must post your contents when your audience is, you know, online.

It won't make sense if you publish your posts according to the LA time if your target audience is in the Central European Time.

You should be privy to your followers' location from your demographics, per city and per Country:

Researching your target audience on Instagram is not a one-time time thing. There's no way you'll be able to figure it at once and go straight into promotion and content creation and would never have to worry about it again.

An Instagram target audience is a continuous process. The more you take your time, the more you learn about your audience – and subsequently, the more targeted and refined your content strategy becomes.

Making Money on Instagram through Brand Collaboration And Sponsorships

Source: Webbizz

As an aspiring influencer, I believe you must be familiar with seeing other influencers' sponsorship posts and stories on your feed most of the time. The amount of money made by influencers through Instagram with every sponsored post, story, and mention for brands is quite lucrative.

A few examples of influencers who have successfully tapped into the gold mine of sponsorship post and weekly income include Instagrammers like Danielle Bernstein who is the owner of We Wore That. In a recent interview with Forbes, she revealed that she makes around $8000 to $20,000 with every Instagram post. With a following of 1.8 million followers on her Instagram page, one can only guess how much she makes off sponsored posts at the moment.

Another notable example is Elma Beganovich. In her interview with Business Insider, the former lawyer claims to make a whopping $20,000 with every post. Her current follower count stands at 697,000.

The rate at which Instagram influencers are moving up the popularity scale and gaining income has left competition like YouTubers, bloggers, and Twitter influencers trying to catch up.

Now, I get the feeling these numbers have you very excited to learn how you can join the elite income earners of Instagram. The completion is insane, and I will be using this comprehensive guide to teach you how to make money with sponsorships from scratch.

Which Influencers Attract Instagram Sponsorships

In layman terms, three main types of influencers earn the big bucks on Instagram. We have the macro influencers who have upwards of 150k followers, the hyper-influencers who have a follower count that ranges between 30k to 150k, and the micro influencers whose follower count few not exceed the 30k mark.

Let's take a more extensive look at each of these categories and the amount of money they get to earn off Instagram sponsorships.

Micro-influencers

Micro influencers are arguably the best of the lot because of their engagement rate on the platform. Micro influencers usually have a quotes fee that ranges around $250-$550 for every Instagram sponsored post according to research by **BlogLovin.**

It does not matter if you can boast of two thousand followers or thirty thousand followers, you can still be regarded as an Instagram influencer as long as you can sway people's opinions and influence their choices. Micro influencers are known for their engagement rates which is why they get Instagram sponsorships from brands easily. Some influencers prefer to promote a brand in exchange for the product they want to influence.

Think of any influencer in your niche, and you can quickly estimate how much they make off Instagram sponsorships need on the basic rate I mentioned earlier. Multiply that amount with the number of brands they influence, and you begin to understand the amount of money they are making.

Hyper-influencers

Influencers who boast of follower counts between 30,000 to 150,000 followers on Instagram are referred to as hyper influencers. These set of influencers charge as much as $1,000 or even more based on which end of the spectrum they belong to follower-wise.

The excellent connection they have with their followers make them very valuable, and they are regarded as experts in their fields. If you want to understand the quality of an influencers engagement fully, check out their profile on **HEEPSY** to get a detailed overview of your favorite influencers profile.

Macro Influencers

Macro influencers are basically celebrities or social media icons with Instagram followers that exceed the 150k mark. They can charge from $10,000 - $25,000 and upwards for a single post or mention. These set of influencers are revered on social media and rank among the most popular people on Instagram. It is very hard to reach this status easily if you are starting as an influencer in 2019.

On the other hand, it is not impossible if you follow the tips explained in this book religiously. The most critical step is to grow your follower base continually. The higher your engagement rate, the higher your chances of getting better pay.

How Do I Get Brand Sponsorship as an Instagram Influencer

Once you have attained any of the follower count marks, the next logical step is to secure brand collaborations. Your level of fame plays a crucial part in this aspect. Collaborating with a brand to earn Instagram sponsorships requires you to be a big name in your niche. There are different ways to secure brand collaboration and earn Instagram. I have highlighted some of these proven techniques below:

1. **Be A Part of Influencer Platforms**

Several influencer platforms on the Internet perform a great job of connecting influencers with paying brands in their niche. Joining any of these influencer marketing platforms is free. You need to sign up and add your details to the database.

These platforms are adept at identifying fake Instagram influencers to lessen the competition which gives you a fresh chance on these platforms. Hence, if you gained your followers by buying bots and other illegal ways, you will definitely be removed. If your followers are real, then you will enjoy operating on these influencer platforms. In no time, you should get picked up by a brand.

2. **Promote Brands In Your Niche**

Many brands are always on the lookout for influencers that tag them for free in their posts. If you fall under this category, they might make you a paid ambassador. It is very easy to perform this action since you already enjoy those products. Get in touch with like-minded influencers and get involved in conversations mentioning the brand.

If such brands find that the traffic you generate for them is substantial, they will be more inclined to collaborate with you. So, go on a crazy brand influencing spree.

3. **Contact Brands via Their Instagram Profiles**

Brands are mindful of their DMs and comments on their Instagram page. One of the quickest ways to catch a brand's attention is to message their page and submit a list of benefits they can get when they partner with you. You can also reach out to them via contact forms or email.

Being a successful Instagram influencer with tons of brand collaboration takes time, and I will further share some tips to help you get to the peak.

Securing your first brand collaboration is a tough ask as you are just starting out, hence your priority should be on maintaining an impressive Instagram profile which requires dedication and hard work.

If you want to be a successful Instagram influencer with a host of brand sponsorships under your belt, remember:

- Be sure to use your Instagram business account so that you can share your Instagram insights with other businesses. You can check a variety of Instagram insights tools if you want to export your Instagram analytics outside the Instagram app.

- Constantly track your follower count and sign up for Unfollowers software to identify any sharp rise or drop in your follower count.

- Registering on a reputable influencer platform tool will guarantee you payment protection in the long run.

- Make use of the proper hashtags to reach your target audience and maximize the potential to gain followers.

- Promote your brand collaboration on Instagram and other social media platforms to earn the brands trust. This action shows you are willing to go over and beyond.

What Brands Want From You In Exchange For Their Money (Sponsorships)

Cultivating a massive following translates to making big money in 2019. Influencer marketing is breaking the status quo and disrupting the generic way through which brand reach out to a new audience. Regular people make big bucks off of sponsored posts now.

Brands require guaranteed reach and engagement from any influencer they collaborate with. Engagement and reach remain the two most essential metrics of any marketing campaign. Reach is the measure of audience size and refers to the number of people who come across a specific post.

Engagement is whenever someone comments on or likes your post. Brands want feedback that shows your content is garnered a high level of engagement and reach. Brands are always willing to at your rate to access your audience.

Research conducted by **MEDIAKIX** indicates that influencer marketing is expected to be a $5-$10 billion industry by 2020. On average, the numbers I have calculated the numbers for paid promotion on Instagram by influencers and Inspo accounts for brands look like this:

Per post:

- 1 million followers: 10,000 likes + 100 comments

- 500 thousand followers: 5000 likes + 20 comments

- 200 thousand followers: 2000 likes + 10 comments

- 100 thousand followers: 1000 likes + 5 comments

- 50 thousand followers: 700 likes + 3 comments

- 20 thousand followers: 500 likes + 1 comment

If your profile generates (on average) these numbers, then you are eligible for paid promotion. These numbers are subject to change for different influencers and niches, but I believe this should be the barest minimum.

At the barest minimum, if you want to be a successful influencer and secure brand sponsorships, you should be hitting the numbers consistently to convince any brand that they will get a good return on their investment.

Brands and companies need the assurance that you can successfully influence your audience to engage with them and click on their profile. This means that it is crucial that you craft top-notch content to get your engagement numbers up with enticing content that your audience can relate with.

This is not an overnight task, as it requires you to spend a minimum of two hours every day to curate high-quality content. Depending on how seriously you take this step, your profile and engagement levels should gain momentum as soon as possible. In time, you won't have to work as hard.

Wherever you find yourself, whenever an idea pops into your mind, be sure to write it down, and perfect it. The best part of creating content is that you can do it from anywhere, just by being on your phone.

When the inquiries start rolling in, and you're replying brand with your rates for services rendered, remember that it would have been a culmination of the effort you have put into being a successful influencer. While it can be time-consuming, there's no denying that once you reach s particular threshold, the reward is far feeder than the work you have put in.

Creating content can also be fun because you're essentially curating stuff that interests you all day. It's your creation. Your own little world.

Comprehensive Guide to Creating an Excellent Influencer Marketing Strategy

A successful influencer marketing strategy is important if you want to connect with new audiences, increase brand exposure, and build authority in your niche. The result of an effective marketing strategy as an influencer leads to new customers for your products and services.

Influencer marketing has many benefits, but it can get confusing to set up, launch, and manage as it usually involves a complicated strategy. Suffice to say, successful influencer marketing strategies are time-consuming. The hurdles associated with launching these strategies have led would-be influencers to quit before they even start.

To get ahead of this rut and successfully carry out an efficient influencer marketing campaign, this chapter will focus on influencer marketing strategy where I will discuss the intricacies of crafting a killer influencer marketing strategy.

Typically, influencers have an extensively engaged audience which gives brands the benefit of getting their product and services across through posts. The exposure helps brands to sell their content in a meaningful, non-generic manner. Gone are the days of door-to-door or cringe-worthy commercials.

A notable of solid influencer marketing is Jada Pinkett Smith partnership with Pantene. By using Jada's profile, Pantene was able to draw the attention of her 5.9 million followers to their brand. Sharing Pantene's message with her audience is the very definition of Influencer marketing.

While I used a celebrity as the case scenario for the definition of influencer marketing strategy here, influencers campaigns do not always utilize the use of celebrities to pass across a brand's message. Influencer marketing strategy can also include industry experts, niche market influencers, and noncompeting brand influencers to promote a successful campaign.

Influencers are all about gaining exposure and promoting a service, but it does not necessarily have to involve the use of Instagram profiles with the largest audience. It involves working with people who have access to a particular target audience hence you should put yourself in a position where brands will connect with you to boost their exposure.

The next part of this book details who the right influencer is and how brands create a successful marketing campaign. I will be writing from a brand's point of view to make sure that you, as an aspiring or growing influencer can understand how brands think and how to strategically position your account and profile to take advantage of this inside information.

Brands that want to launch a successful influencer marketing strategy should take this next part of my attorney very seriously.

How to Create an Influencer Marketing Strategy

The following steps have been streamlined to help you successfully create and launch an effective influencer strategy for your brand.

Set Your Goals

Like any sensible marketing plan, it is important to outline your goal and determine what you want to achieve from this campaign. When you define your goals from the beginning of the planning stage, it affords you the ability to shape a working strategy going forward. This will also provide you an idea of the particular metrics to track and monitor, to determine the level of success at the end of the campaign.

The most important goals you should consider in your influencer marketing strategy are:

- **Brand Awareness:** Multiplying the number of people that are aware of and like the brand

- **Creating Brand Identity:** Getting more people to understand your brand's values and personality

- **Audience Building:** Increasing your brand followers and subscribers

- **Engagement:** Getting more likes, comments, and shares for your content

- **Lead Generation:** Ensuring an additional number of people sign up for offers and lead magnets

- **Sales:** Securing an increased number is sales on products and services

- **Customer Loyalty:** Maintaining interest and customer connection with your brand

- **Link Building:** Increasing the number of backlinks to your website

Picking A Preferred Type of Influencer Marketing Campaign

Once you have successfully highlighted your goals, it is time to pick the type of Influencer marketing campaign that is best suited to help you accomplish your mission. Usually, influencer marketing campaigns are categorized into three forms of relationship triggers: Inspire, Hire, or both.

You can inspire an influencer to promote your content or messaging of their own volition (which I mentioned earlier as one of the best ways to get brands to notice you as an upcoming influencer). You can also decide to pay influencers to promote your brand. In some situations, a mix of both strategies is the way to go.

I have highlighted some of the best influencer marketing strategies to employ you should consider for your brand:

- **Gifting:** Sensing frees products and offering services to an influencer in exchange for a mention or review

- **Guest Posting:** Contributing content to influencer blogs

- **Sponsored Content:** Paying an influencer to write about your rand on their blog or social channel. You can create the content yourself or outsource it to people who understand the audience better

- **Creating Content Together:** Forming a partnership with an influencer to curate content that will be published in your website or a third-party site

- **Social Media Mentions:** This strategy involves hiring a social media personality or celebrity to mention your brand and post your content

- **Giveaways and Contests**: Running a contest where an influencer in your niche distributes prizes with their followers

- **Influencers Takeover:** Big brands like MTV, Netflix, and other use this strategy where an influencer takes control of all social media accounts for a stipulated amount of time, especially during events or the launch of a product

- **Affiliates:** Providing Influencers with a code to drive sales. They get a percentage on the number of sales they make through their followers

- **Discount code:** Providing an influencer with a unique promo code for products that they can offer to their audience

- **Brand Ambassadors:** Identify loyal brand fans who will mention your products and services on their Instagram page in exchange for free products, exclusive offers, or being featured by your company

While these marketing strategies are not fixed or guaranteed to fulfill your criteria, they are flexible enough to be used generally and add up to create a successful influencer marketing strategy.

When creating your marketing plan, be sure to include at least two of these tips to create your customized influencer marketing strategy that appears to your audience and promotes your brand.

Identify and Define Your Audience

Once you have outlined your goals and created a custom influencer marketing strategy that works best for you, you still need a few things before hiring or partnering with influencers. Before you can choose the right person to help you connect with your target audience, you need to identify and define who you want to sell your service to.

Prior to the time when you search for influencers, take your time to outline specific details about the target audience you want to gain access to with through your marketing campaign. A good way to achieve that is by creating a buyer persona that combines both psychographic and demographic segmentation. Once you identify your audience, it will be easier to choose the right people that can get you access to that audience.

Find the Right Influencers

An effective way to identify influencers in your niche that can help you reach your audience is by using Alexa's Audience Overlap Tool. Simply input the URL of websites that have the same audience you're trying to reach. The tool will respond with a list of websites in the same niche that shares the same audience.

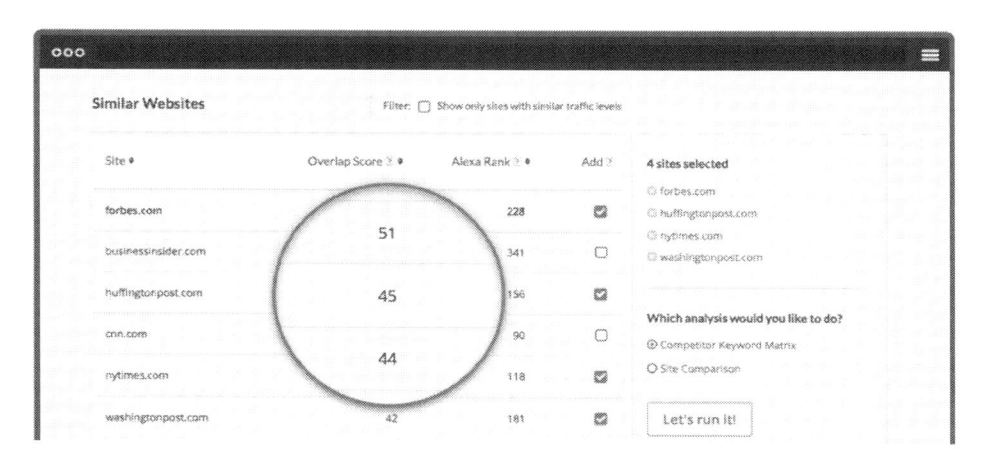

This helps you to identify websites that you can guest blog on as you know these sites have a similar audience to the ones you want to reach. Therefore, they would be a great place to curate and share your content.

For example, if your brand sells online courses on leadership, your target audience could possibly read michalhyatt.com. Copy the URL into the audience overlap tool to find other sites that your audience also visit. This list of sites should serve as a guide for finding the right influencers who can contribute to the success of your campaign.

Find Influencers using Backlinks

Another effective method of identifying the best influencers is by using Alexa's Competitor Backlink Checker. Copy ten sites from the Overlap tool and paste them in the backlinks checker. Then, run the program.

The report should show all the links that are pointing to your list of sites. This list can be used to find sites that are approachable and sites with the highest traffic regarding affiliate tags. These sites already worked with your competitors so they should be willing to promote your brand too.

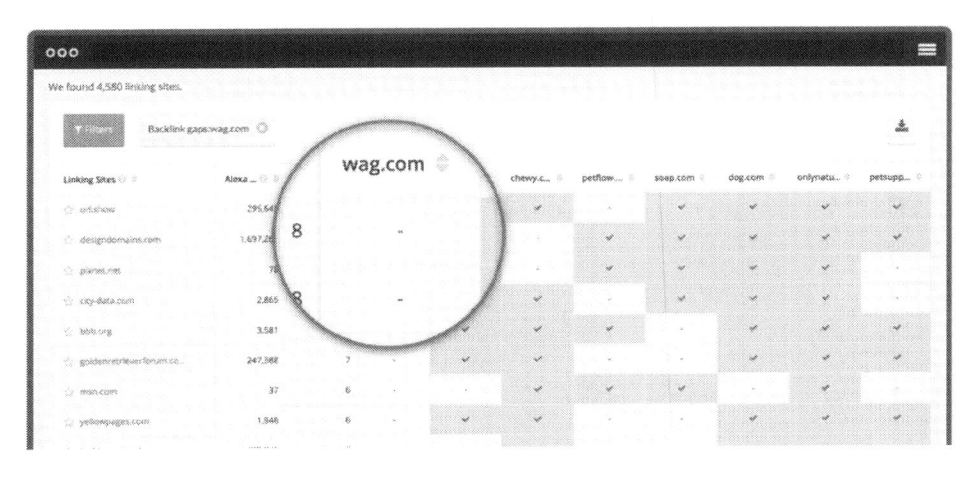

A good example is michaelhyatt.com, and it's competitors, when researching backlinks in this niche, you will notice that personalsuccesstoday.com is linked to at least five of these sites. This shows that it is one of the most formidable websites in that particular niche and you should partner with them as part of your influencer marketing strategy.

Clicking through backlinks will present you with an overview of the type of content that each site publishes, including mentions and guest posts, so you can create a solid outreach plan.

Find Influencers by Topics

If you are not familiar with sites or competitors that target the audience in your niche, Alexa's keyword Share of Voice Tool can be used to find the right influencers. Search for a popular term related to your industry or a specific topic you want to gain influence on. The report should provide a list of sites that have a major influence on that term, which means that these sites possess a lot of online visibility for that phrase.

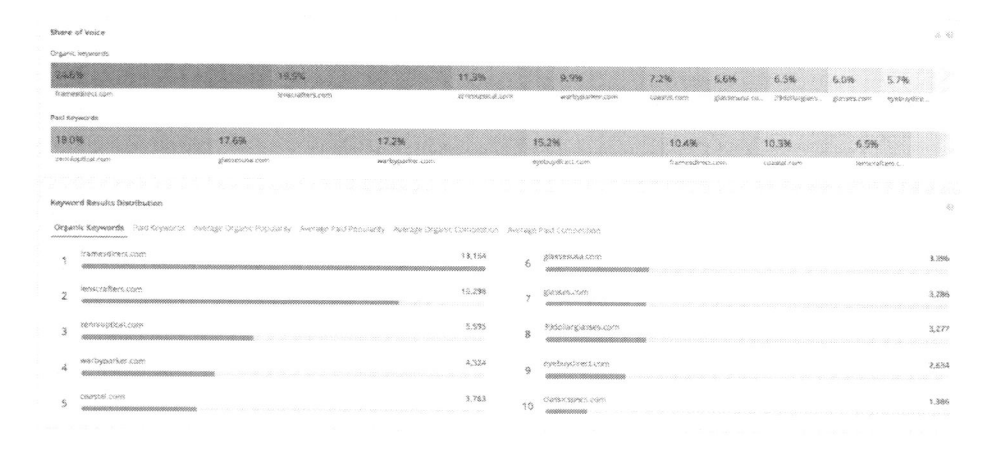

To find companies or brands that are a figure of authority in the niche you want to influence in, your best bet is to use the Share of Voice Tool to discover websites that attract traffic for that phrase.

For an influencer, make yourself available by afflicting yourself with the popular websites. And now since you know how brands search for influencers, use this knowledge to make your profile available where necessary.

Numerous tools and methods can be used to find influencers. You can search for relevant hashtags on Instagram and other social platforms to find the most relevant influencers in your niche, or more specifically, ones that have an audience that you're looking to influence.

Any of these tools are very useful for identifying blogging and social media influencers. First off is BuzzSumo, NinjaOutreach, Klout, Klear, Deep Social, BuzzStream, and Izea.

Qualify Your Influencers

Don't fall into the trap of over-excitement when it is time to find influencers. Before you start your outreach, you need to be sure they are the right fit for your goals and your brand. Qualify your audience. It is more beneficial to partner with an influencer who has a small audience that is concentrated with your target market than to work with one who has an extensive audience that has fee people you want to get access to.

Hence, don't place priority on the size of the audience. Rather, you should focus on working with an influencer who is the audience you want to reach.

Remember the right audience is key to a successful influencer marketing campaign.

As an influencer, one of the best ways to assess your audience interests is to use Alexa's Audience Overlap Tool. Check out different websites and review trends to find out what the latest points of interest of your audience.

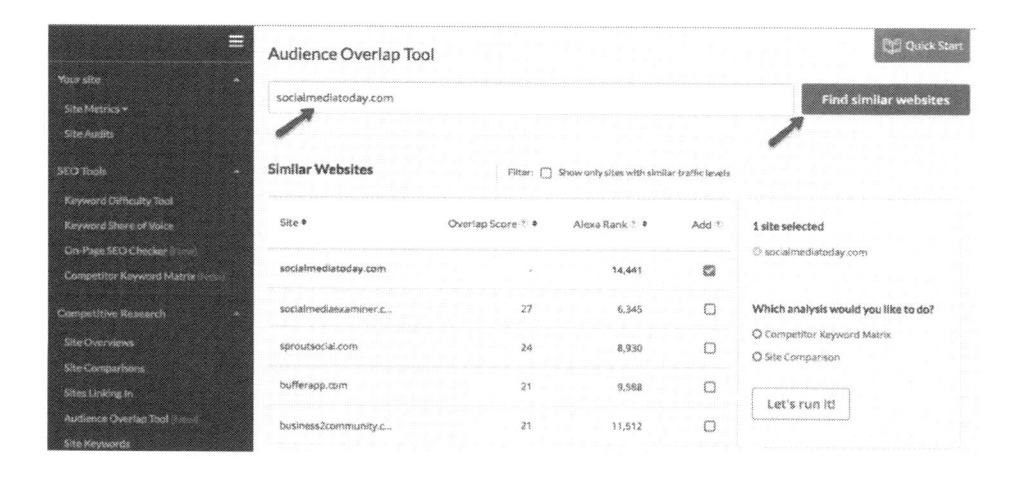

By checking out the websites your audience frequently visits, you can tailor your content to match their interests on Instagram. Not only Wil your followers appreciate your content but also, when brands search for specific latest trends your profile will come up.

Think like a brand if you want to be noticed by a brand.

Checking the sites your audience visit will tell you a lot your audience identity habits, and needs.

Reach, and authority is also an important metric when it comes to gauging the viability of an influencer. Quality of audience engagement is an important metric, but you must not overlook the size of the audience.

For social media accounts, brands usually check the number of followers and engagement numbers with their posts. Target influencers who have a constantly engaged audience that comment and like on the influencer posts. As an influencer, take note of this.

For your brand, if you're looking to engage influencers that operate on blogs and website, check out their on-site metrics. This is where Alexa's Site Overview Tool comes in handy. The software helps you to identify different metrics related to bounce rate, page views, number of backlinks, number of visitors, time on site, and the Alexa rank that pinpoints the authority of the site in its niche.

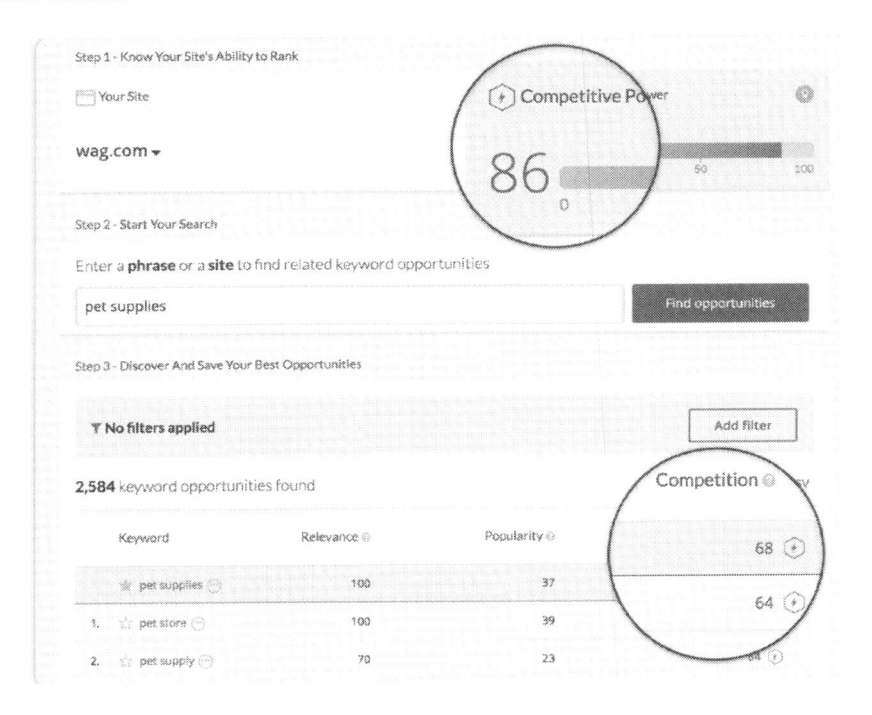

In your influencer marketing strategy, qualify the messaging and the content. You should continually strive to work with influencers that align with your brand. Research the type of content that the influencer tends to share in their platform and how it relates to your brand and business. Due diligence is important.

Religiously go through their posts, web content, and status updates to make sure it;

- Is relevant to your industry, brand, product, and services

- Is of top-notch quality and contains content that resonates with the values of your brand

- Mirrors the values and ideals of your brand and that it resonates with the core values of your company

Another important part of your influencer marketing strategy is the ability to come up with content that influencers cannot refuse. If your influencer marketing strategy involves creating content or guest posting on an influencer Instagram feed, then your biggest chance of success is to create content that speaks to the influencer and by extension, their audience.

To create engaging content, it is essential to develop ideas that target keywords and hashtags.

Finding the top keyword that attracts the highest engagement is no easy task, and I recommend that you utilize Alexa's Keyword Difficulty Tool for this task. Enter a phrase or hashtag related to any niche of your choosing and select low-competition keywords that pop up frequently on the Explore tab.

This approach is very useful and allows you to deliver content that is tailor-made for your influencer audiences.

As an influencer, you can employ these tactics when hired by a brand to differentiate yourself from the competition and attract the highest engagements. Ideally, the result should be increased brand exposure and traffic to the brand's website.

One of the effective ways to generate content on a consistent basis is by researching Alexa's Competitive Keyword Matrix. This tool is straightforward to use. Simply fill in the name of the influencers site alongside their major competitors, and use the filter feature to generate organic keyword gaps for the site you want to sell your services on.

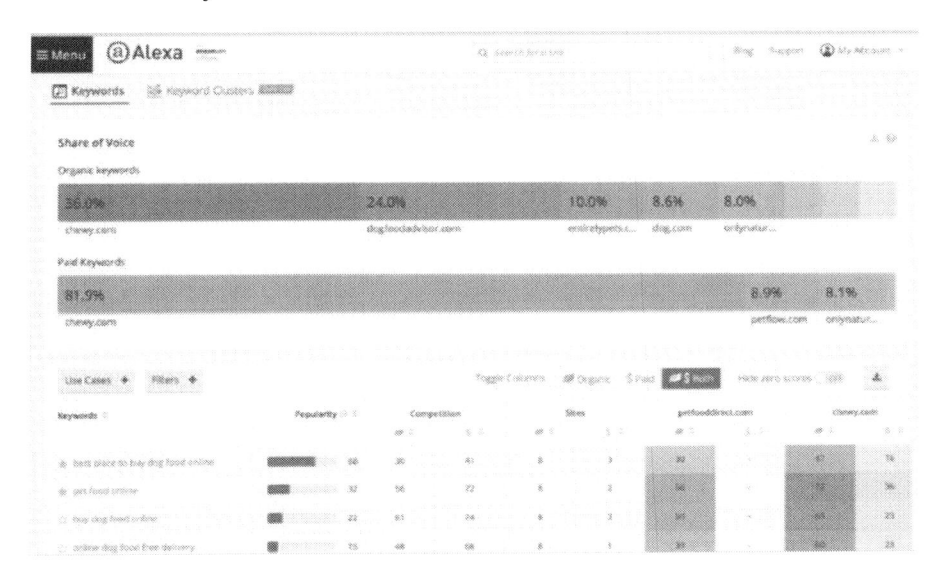

Alexa's Competitive Keyword Matrix is an impressive tool that generates a report of the keywords that attract traffic to other sites, but not the primary site. You can view the topics that your competitors focus on that you have not yet jumped on. This information is bound to elicit new ideas for guest post topics that can be used by the influencer. (As an influencer, you can take charge of this task and provide insight whenever you pitch your ideas to brands)

As your audience is already defined, you can now start looking for influencers who can help you achieve your goals in your bid to connect with your target market.

For a successful influencer marketing campaign that is not limited to Instagram, you should explore the following categories of influencers;

- Social Media stars

- Industry experts

- Bloggers

- Noncompeting brands

- Celebrities

- Customers - Brand Ambassadors

Once you have pinpointed the type of Influencer, you wish to partner with, start searching for brands and individuals that fit that criterion. After you have chosen a suitable influencer that can relate to the objectives of your brand, the next step is to agree on the design of your marketing campaign.

As this is a collaboration, there are bound to be difficulties possibly due to miscommunication and differences in idea execution. Your objective as a brand is to pass your message across in an attractive problem-solving manner through your influencer marketing strategy. The objective of an influencer is to take your content, refurbish it, and make sure it is presented in a quality non-generic manner that will appeal to the audience.

It is essential to make sure you do not lose your tone or uniqueness as a brand. To make the process easier, the brand and influencer must collaborate to come up with a definite use of what the brand goals are and how to achieve them without sacrificing the originality associated with the influencer Instagram page.

As mentioned earlier, this is why it is essential (as a brand) to bring up qualitative suggestions that the influencer cannot refuse.

One of the most important results from recent influencer studies is that a lot of influencers find it very valuable when they collaborate with brands regarding passing a message across instead of working solo. This helps them to work well within guidelines set by the brand. Employing this tactic leads to a precise execution of goals.

Provide the influencers with essential details that can't be gotten from other sources – such as product history and brand trivia, as well as sources like product photo or even access to a member of the production staff. However, this does not mean that the influencer is free to post messages on behalf of the brand whenever they wish. Every message posted on their social media platform must be a result of a collaborative process.

Working together involves combining forces and taking the best ideas from both the brand and influencer to produce a solid end product. The influencer understands the audience and is great at appealing to their narrative while the brand understands the intricacies of the products and benefits involved.

A 2018 study by LaunchMetrics showed that 63% of influencers claimed that their foremost motivation when collaborating with a company was "valuable content for my brand." This proves that influencers value the process of content collaboration.

Content creation is a very tasking process nowadays, and there is a growing demand for new content by the audience. This is where you can take advantage as a brand. By being creative and offering the audience original and fresh content, you can provide the services that will be irresistible to them. The collaboration between an influencer and a brand is aimed at developing a winning situation for both entities on a professional level.

Best Tips To Achieve A Successful Influencer Marketing Campaign

While we have discussed the elements needed to build and maintain a successful influencer marketing campaign, the onus is on me to add to explore additional tips that are working in 2019.

STEP BY STEP GUIDE: INFLUENCER MARKETING
Influencer Marketing is about engaging influencers to create content that moves audiences to action

1. **DEFINE OBJECTIVE & TARGET** — Who/When, production profile, and outcome
2. **IDENTIFY & BRIEF INFLUENCERS** — Audience, tone and brand fit
3. **INFLUENCERS CREATE & AMPLIFY FTC COMPLIANT CONTENT**
4. **MONITOR & ID BEST PERFORMING CONTENT** — Most engagement, likes, comments, shares
5. **OPTIMIZE & "TURN ON THE GAS"** — Paid distribution of best performing content
6. **MEASURE & BENCHMARK**

www.shespeaksinc.com

Designing the Campaign

As mentioned earlier, your entire influencer marketing strategy is dependent on the central campaign objective. Once you have defined goals, the rest of the strategy must be tailored towards developing the strategy.

One of the essential elements to factor in is the budget of your campaign. Firstly, you need to determine the amount of money you are willing to invest before thinking about any potential income. It is crucial to note the cost of the campaign will also include the following:

- Product samples
- Special promotions for the public
- Research
- Cost of strategy planning

More than six percent of the brands approached by **LaunchMetrics** in the study claimed that they expect their marketing budgets to rise over the next 12 months exponentially.

Back to you. Is your budget growing? Are you selling different messages through your campaign or focused on a single one? Are you looking to collaborate with lots of micro-influencers or a big name macro influencer? Do you have the time and technical know-how needed to create campaign content?

When it comes to influencer marketing strategy, the majority of brands choose to send a product sample to the influencer and expect a post on the product. In the short term, this method of collaboration is doomed to fail and will lead to disappointing results. However, on the flip side, it is great for products that require spontaneity.

An alternate but equally effective way of collaborating is to plan a campaign that will stand the test of time. Sustainability is a crucial feature of any influencer marketing campaign mad should be prioritized. A notable example is fashion campaigns. In this niche, the most successful brands usually map out their campaign month before the launch of a product line, including all seasons and the various collections for the upcoming year, as their primary focus.

You need to decide the type of content you expect to get from your influencers. There is a variety of content that influencers can create: sponsored posts, event hosting, affiliate links, and social media promotion.

Sponsored content remains the most requested influencer service s more than 85% of influencers operate via sponsored content. However, you do not necessarily have to jump on this bandwagon. Your mode of operation depends on your goals. Don't just sign up for sponsored posts with your influencer because you hear it works. Make sure you understand how it works, it's the purpose, and if it is the best fit for your brand and your products.

Taking your time to answer these questions will help you achieve actual results rather than just claiming you have executed an influencer marketing strategy.

But what type of content do you desire from your influencers? Affiliate links? Event hosting? Sponsored posts? Promotion on social media?

Creating Content Together

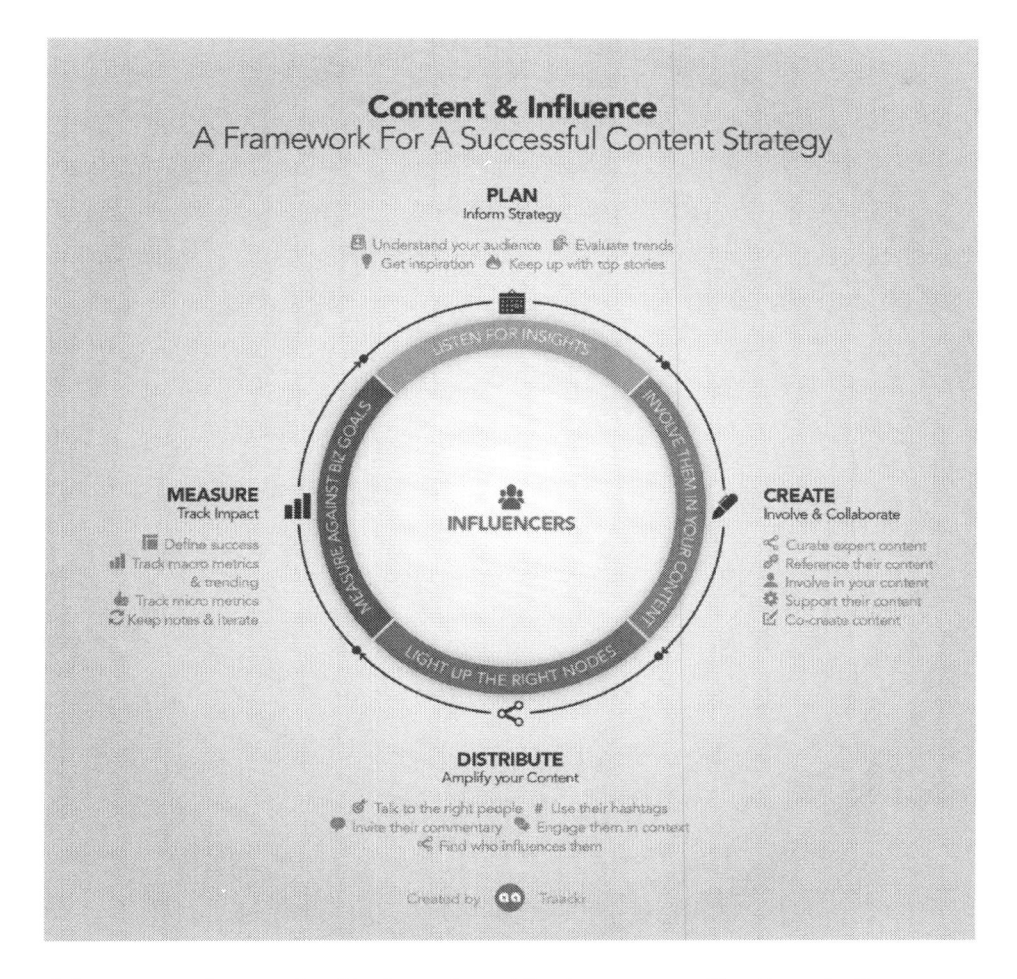

Content & Influence
A Framework For A Successful Content Strategy

PLAN
Inform Strategy
- Understand your audience
- Evaluate trends
- Get inspiration
- Keep up with top stories

CREATE
Involve & Collaborate
- Curate expert content
- Reference their content
- Involve in your content
- Support their content
- Co-create content

DISTRIBUTE
Amplify your Content
- Talk to the right people
- Use their hashtags
- Invite their commentary
- Engage them in context
- Find who influences them

MEASURE
Track Impact
- Define success
- Track macro metrics & trending
- Track micro metrics
- Keep notes & iterate

INFLUENCERS

LISTEN FOR INSIGHTS · INVOLVE THEM IN YOUR CONTENT · LIGHT UP THE RIGHT NODES · MEASURE AGAINST BIZ GOALS

Created by Traackr

After you have drafted and settled on an effective influencer marketing strategy, including the duration of the program (number of posts in a daily, weekly, or monthly basis), co-creating the content is the next step in your campaign.

This part of the influencer marketing campaign is here you decide what every post must include and the message to be passed across to the audience. It also involves planning how the content will evolve over a period.

Understandably, this will test the compatibility level of the influencer and the brand and how they can work as a team. Together, you must work on creating effective messages that speak to a chosen demographic and fulfills the brand's objectives. The content must be written in a way that fits in perfectly with the usual content on the influencers feed. This is a critical aspect of creating content – making sure that your brand content fits in seamlessly with typical content in your niche – although there are other essential details to consider.

While the average consumer has learned to ignore generic messages on social media and turn a blind to brand banners online, an effective marketing strategy ensures that your content is not overridden with logos and offers. This means that messages in this niche do not have to be eye-catching or overly creative. Instead, it needs to fit on with the influencer's profile, to provide the audience with a topic they want to discuss and share.

Executing the Campaign

If you have reached this stage, then that means you have taken care of everything else in the campaign. The big question is: what next?

Don't even consider resting on your laurels or dump so the work on the influencer while you wait for results. Research conducted by Neoreach.com confirms that brands need to conduct detailed tracking of the campaign's progress to get figures that will help you ascertain your level of progress and can be used as a metric for measurement.

First off, you need to create a spreadsheet to save the tracked data. There are many programs and software that can perform this task efficiently. If you do not have the workforce or time to monitor the tracking process, you should outsource this task to a professional team that monitors your campaign process and all relevant data associated with your influencer marketing strategy.

	A	B	C	D
1		Followers	Impressions	Traffic
2	Influencer 1	10,000		
3	Post a		2000	200
4	Post b		4000	300
5	Post c		3000	150
6				
7	Influencer 2	30,000		
8	Post a		7000	400
9	Post b		5000	350
10	Post c		10000	750
11				

You also need to track the reaction of the audience to your content and actions of the campaign, including taking screenshots of the whole process. The truth is, they will be very useful in the long run.

Measuring Effectiveness

Measuring the effectiveness of your campaign remains an essential step for any successful campaign. This action will enlighten you on whether your efforts are paying off and the aspects of your campaign that need improvement. Executing a campaign without constantly measuring the results is wasting half of your time and effort.

NOW: Measure Effective Influence

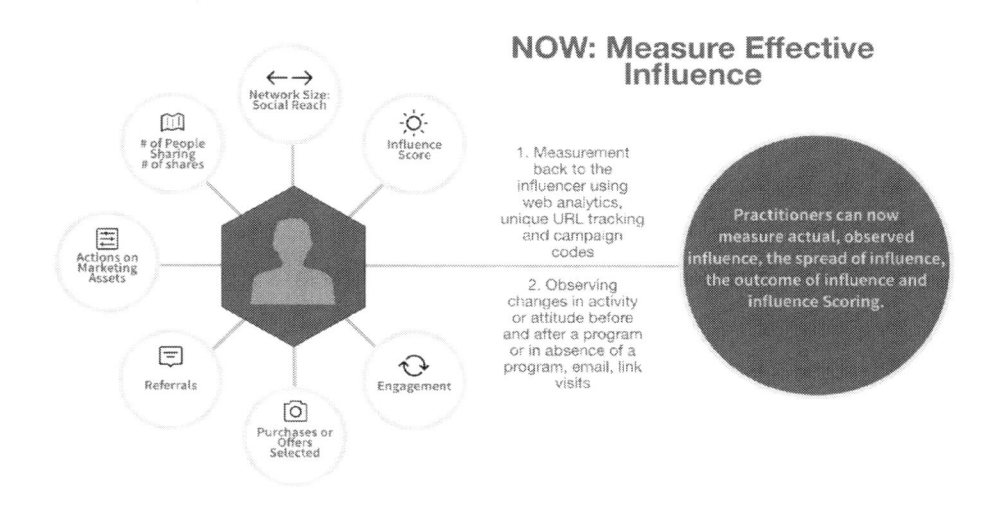

- Network Size: Social Reach
- # of People Sharing # of shares
- Influence Score
- Actions on Marketing Assets
- Referrals
- Engagement
- Purchases or Offers Selected

1. Measurement back to the influencer using web analytics, unique URL tracking and campaign codes

2. Observing changes in activity or attitude before and after a program or in absence of a program, email, link visits

Practitioners can now measure actual, observed influence, the spread of influence, the outcome of influence and Influence Scoring.

The Word of Mouth Marketing Association (WOMMA) reiterates that every campaign has two levels of measurement:

- The potential to influence
- The reaction to the influence

Before and throughout your influencer marketing campaign, there are five critical factors to consider which are:

A. Total Investment

Earlier, I discussed the importance of monitoring the budget of your campaign. Now that you have launched your campaign, it is imperative to check back and confirm that the projected figure for your budget is still the same for your investment or if extra costs were incurred during the preparation of the campaign.

With all these details, you can then ascertain if you have received an adequate return on your investment and the extent to which your brand has gained from the campaign.

B. Reach and Gain

Reach is calculated as the number of individuals you want to influence – in this case, and it means the number of followers on your influencer's Instagram account. , on the other hand, refers to the gain for the brand in comparison to the investment made which is gotten by calculating the number of page impressions, sales conversion rates, and increase in engagement.

Once you have calculated these figures, it is time to calculate further the ration added. This is based on the initial reach your brand had and your initial objectives, that way you can ascertain whether your influencer campaign was useful for your brand and if they fulfilled the goals you set out to achieve with your campaign.

Remember to pay attention to the feedback you get from your campaign. An excellent tool to perform this croon is **Traackr.** Traackr monitors engagements and increases in impressions for brand exposure before the start of the campaign to the end of the campaign.

C. Human Feelings Towards Your Brand

While the ultimate goal of any influencer marketing campaign is sales conversion, there are several ways through which you can achieve this goal. Monitoring the public's disposition towards your brand and how your target audience reacts to your campaign is crucial if you want to attract a wider demographic and record a higher sales conversion.

It also affords you the chance to pinpoint any shortcomings in your brand's communication while at the same time identifying the more excellent points of your campaign. Tools that monitor audience feelings towards a particular brand include **People Browsr** and **Meltwater**.

D. The Effect Of Your Message On The Brand

To calculate the effect your campaign message has had on your brand, variables such as the number of mentions for your brand, generation of online traffic, number of followers on social media profiles, and number of subscribers need to be evaluated.

E. New Sales

This is outright the most important ensure of a successful influencer marketing campaign for any brand, or at least most brands. It is important to note that sales derived from your campaign might not trip in immediately or during the campaign. Be sure to check for data even after you end the campaign constantly.

F. Repeating Your Winning Formula

Practice makes perfect. I can guarantee that the steps highlighted, including the tips make up the recipe for a successful influencer marketing campaign. Make sure you treat the processes as much as you can to double and triple both your conversion rates and sales.

The better you define your goals, the clearer your path to success.

The Future of Influencer Marketing

Influencer marketing over the past few years has overshadowed contemporary forms of marketing. An influencer marketing campaign is the go-to for most brands, and more people are becoming influencers every passing day without watering down the effect of influencer marketing on social media platforms.

I will briefly discuss the future of influencer marketing in three points. Here goes:

1. **Influential Profiles Will Operate On A Lower Scale Level**

Majority of brands in the near future will stop collaborating with major influencer accounts with an outrageous amount of followers. Instead, the focus will be on identifying a targeted audience even if it means a lot less brand exposure.

Finding a micro influencer who is more connected to their followers is the growing priority for brands, and as an upcoming influencer, you need to prioritize your current audience over gaining more followers. Many professionals had claimed that they achieved better results when they worked with small-time influencers.

2. **Organic Messages Are Coming Back**

Natural interactions will always trump programmed sponsored content. In the future, brand communication that seems less prepared and more natural will sell better with the audience. Influencers who operate on a small scale and interact with their followers can communicate their message reliably and. As an influencer, constantly interact with your followers as this builds a connection. This connection will come in handy when you advertise a product or service.

3. Influencers Will Take Creative Control Of Posts

A major problem in influencer marketing strategy campaigns in 2019 is the difference in opinions between brand and influencers. I fully expect influencers to take charge as designers and deliveries of content in the future. They understand the audience and are best suited to tailor the brand messages to their followers.

That isn't all. Once brands witness the impact that small scale influencers have and their influence on the way their message is released to the public, they will learn to appreciate the value of natural interactions. The value that an everyday individual has on the way their fellow audience views a brand cannot be overemphasized.

Once an individual makes a brand of their daily lives and continually sells that brand to a target audience, influencer marketing will transform into an automatic system which frequently rewards individuals for promoting their favorite brands, regardless of audience size.

Influencer Marketing Research Tools

In this section, we will discuss the importance of influencer marketing research tools and how to perform crucial steps associated with the success of an influencer campaign. To start with, I have highlighted three important aspects of tracking a successful influencer marketing research.

- **Acquiring Competitor Keywords**

Conducting extensive research and understanding what an influencer website needs helps you to have a better opportunity to secure guest blogging positions where you can collaborate and share content on sites.

- **Track Your Outreach**

When you start your social media influencing or guest blogging campaign, it is crucial to keep things organized. It is very to lose opportunities and the chance to collaborate with an influencer due to an unprofessional influencer marketing strategy structure. A good example is when different members of your team reach out to the same influencer with different emails. It shows that your brand is not in sync.

Develop a comprehensive system for staying updated. An excellent way to perform this action is by creating a document that tracks every step of your campaign. An ideal template should look like this;

A. Who reached out to the influencer

B. When did they reach out

C. Which Influencers was contacted

D. Notes about the communication

E. Plans for a follow-up

F. Status of the outreach

- **Track and Analyze Your Results**

When you close your influencer marketing campaign, every single mention and profile share on social media platforms feels like a victory and justification of your investment. Simply having an influencer promote your brand or may your message isn't a sign of success. That is the basic requirement.

The real metric for judging the success of a campaign is the goals achieved.

It is very simple to calculate if you have reached your goals, track and measure the results of your campaign. There are different metrics to measure the success of your influencer marketing campaign, depending on your initial marketing objectives.

- **Brand awareness metric:** page views, site users, time on site, website traffic, social mentions

- **Building brand identity metric:** PR coverage, social mentions, number of affiliate links

- **Engagement metric:** comments, likes, and shares

- **Lead Generation metric:** opt-ins

- **Customer loyalty metric:** renewal rates, customer retention rates

- **Sales metric:** revenue changes, new sales, price per ticket

- **Link building metric**: quality of links, number of links

Track the data for each metric on your influencer marketing campaign so that you can take note of the strategies that thrived as the flops. This data Wil be critical to the success of your next influencer marketing strategy. Make sure you repeat the processes that worked and ignore the strategies that do not conform to your brand's objectives.

Joining The Influencer Community: Best Platforms For Any Influencer

As an influencer, marketing yourself outside of Instagram is crucial to the success of your brand. Finding the right platform to showcase your skills can be tough which is why I have listed the best influencer marketing platforms.

Brands visit these sites to hire the best influencers in their niche, and you can take advantage of this knowledge to secure big contracts with the value to you add to their brand. The right automated platforms can equip you with the tools needed to get your big break and cement your position as a leading influencer in your niche.

Upfluence

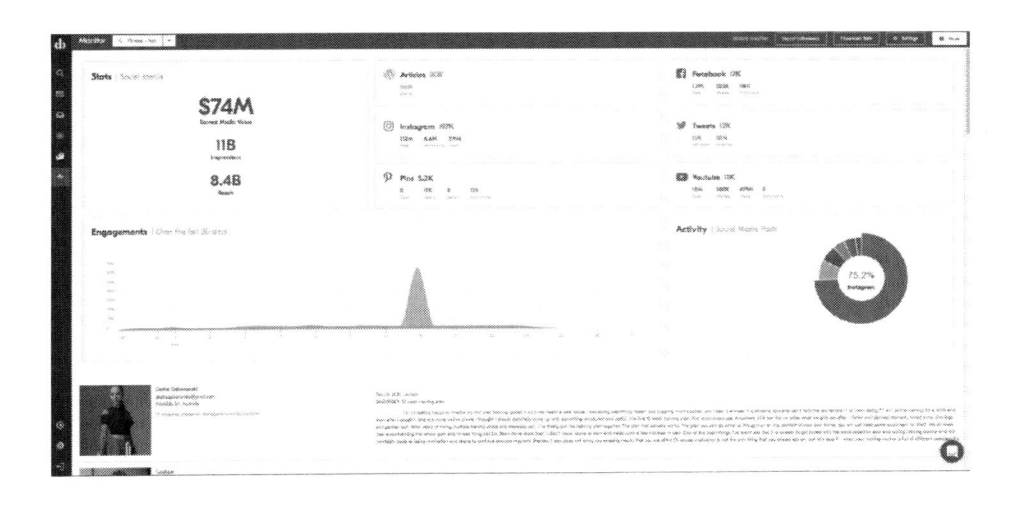

Upfluence provides an extensive database with their monthly subscription in addition to the ability to access influencers from a general dashboard where you can measure results of campaigns on Instagram, Facebook, Twitter, Pinterest, and blogs. Big names like Microsoft and PayPal hire influencers from this platform.

Revfluence

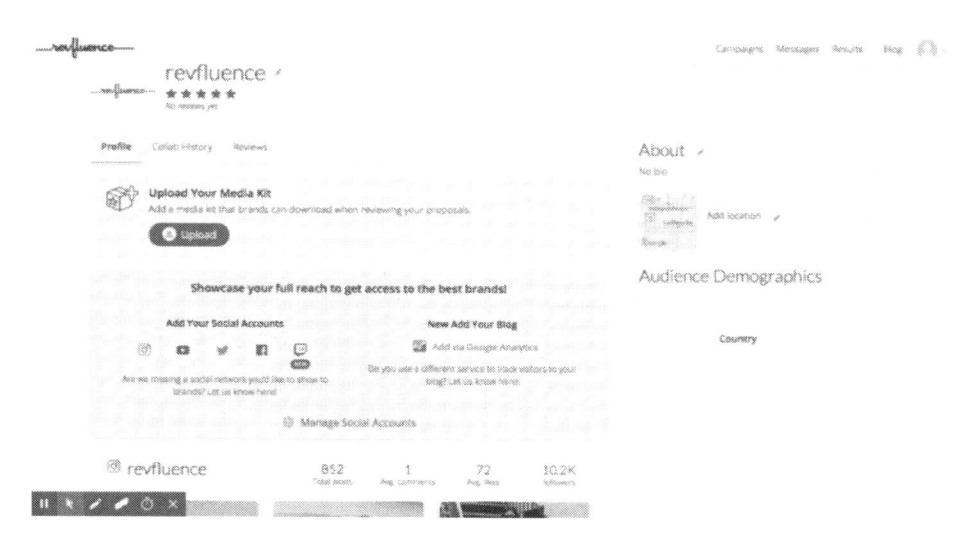

Revfluence is the go-to platform for brands that want to boost their exposure and scale their programs. The site provides analytics tools and a suite of influencer discovery. Priority is placed on influencer relationship management system which serves as one of the key filters that allow marketers to manage as many influencers as they can at any given time.

FameBit

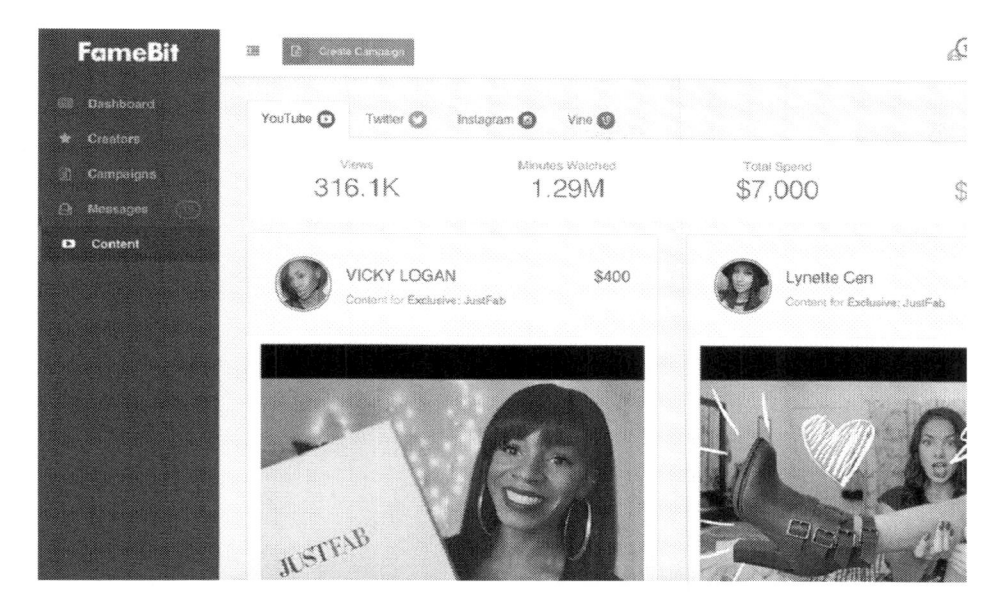

FameBit was acquired by Google in October 2016, and the site works by providing brands with a platform to post a campaign and influencers can then pitch ideas on how to execute them. This means brands need to post a campaign and can expect different influencers from various platforms to bid for the project.

Traackr

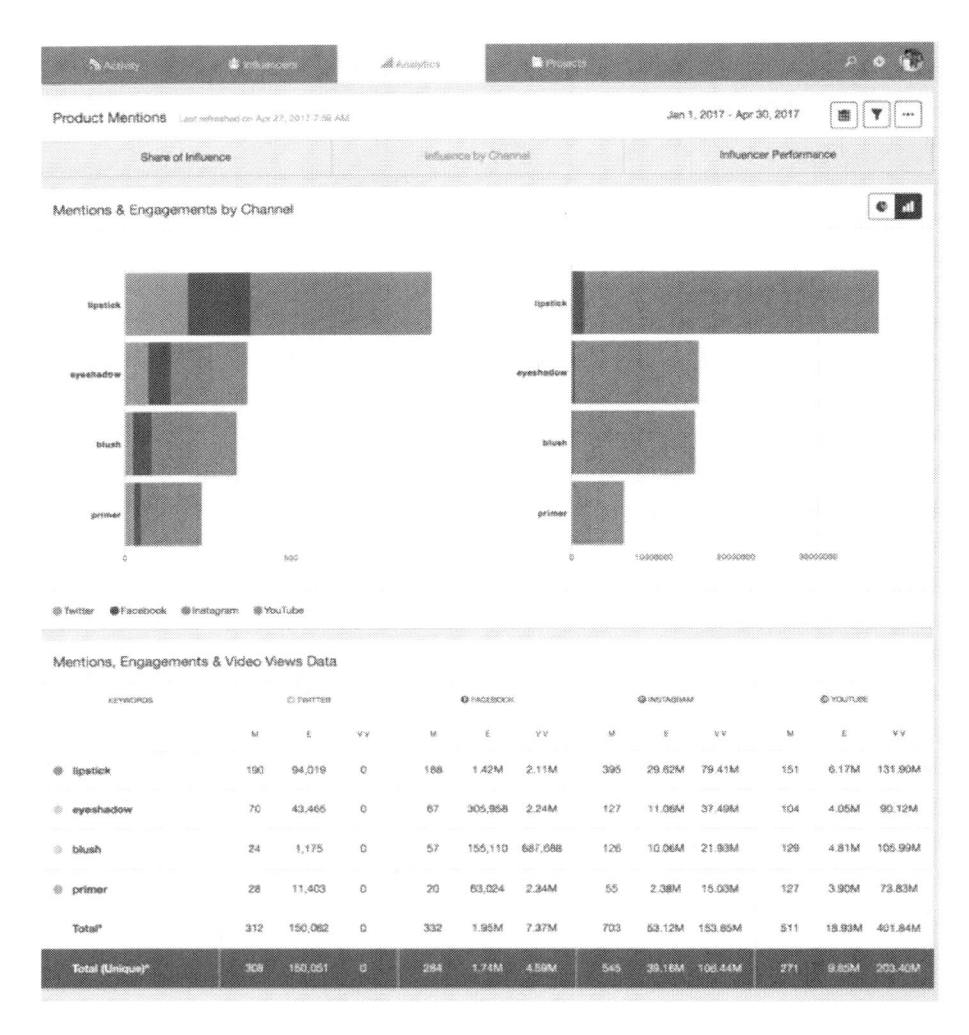

Traackr remains one of the most prominent influencer marketing platforms since its establishment in 2008. Users get unfettered access to a database of influencers on Traackr on a variety of platforms including Instagram, YouTube, Twitter, Facebook, Pinterest, Tumblr, and blogs, as well as campaign management and relationship management.

IZEA

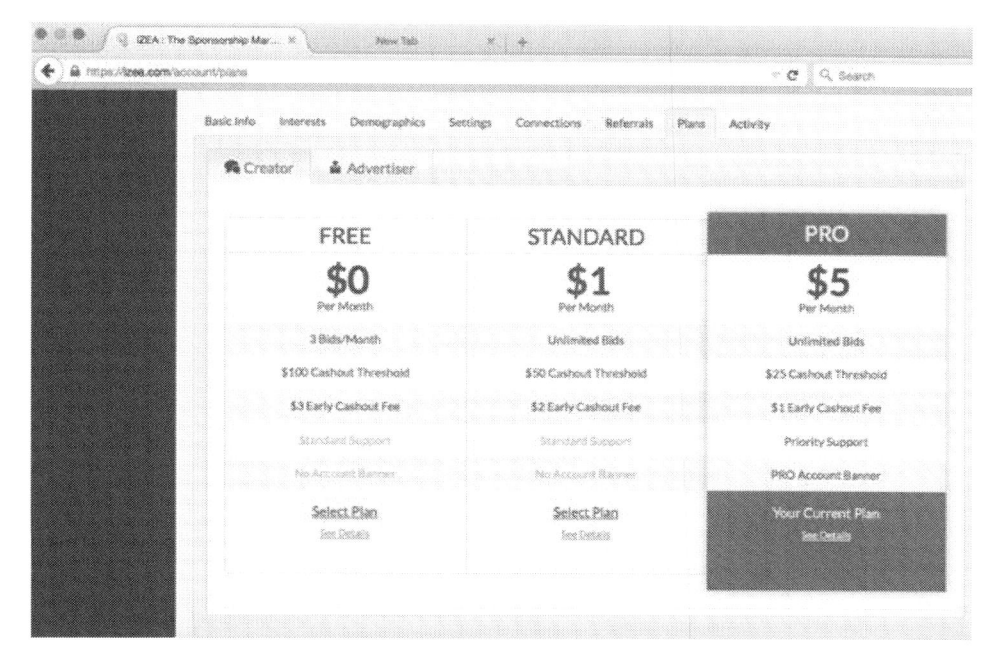

IZEA has been a giant in the influencer marketing industry as far back as 2006. They provide both forward and services for agencies and brands who are interested in entering the influencer marketing niche. The site is unique with the variety of content they provide, ranging from long-form content written by established journalists to short media posts by Instagram baddies.

Julius

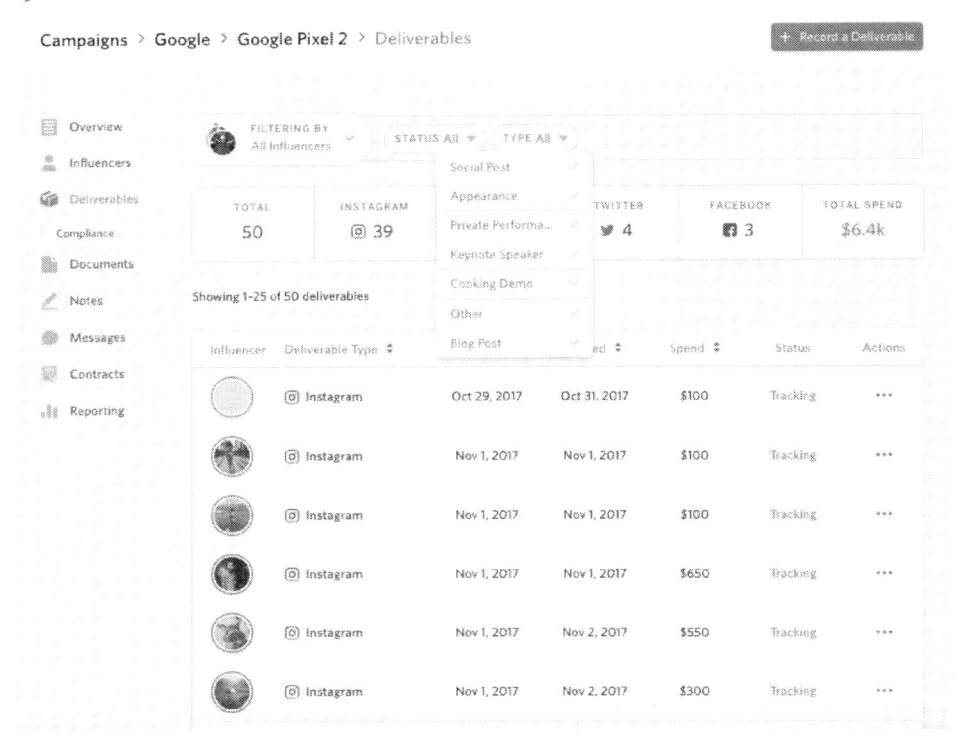

Julius prides itself on being a "100% Vetted" platform that caters for influencer marketing. But isn't that what every influencer marketing platform claims? Julius bucks that claim up as every influencer is reviewed by a human being, not an algorithm. Founded by Tiki Barber – yes, the NFL legend – brands can run campaigns in Instagram, Twitter, Facebook, Snapchat, YouTube, and Pinterest through this site.

Klear

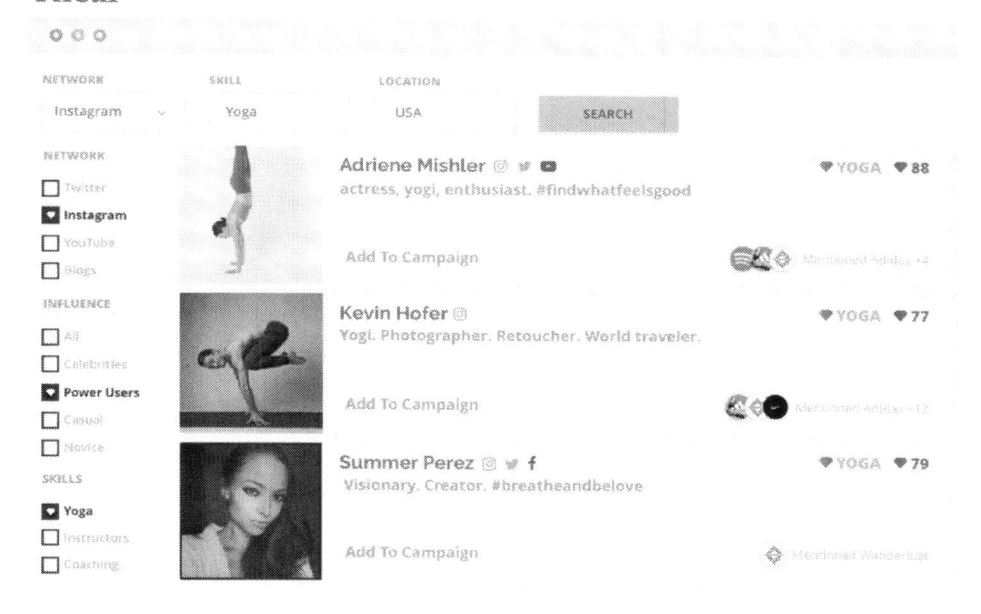

Klear provides an interesting mix of upwards of 500 million profiles complete with historical data, grouped into different categories. Klear provides access to influencer marketing campaigns across Instagram, YouTube, Twitter, and blogs. Overall, even though it is more suited to agencies and enterprise-level brands, there is a starter plan available.

Mustr

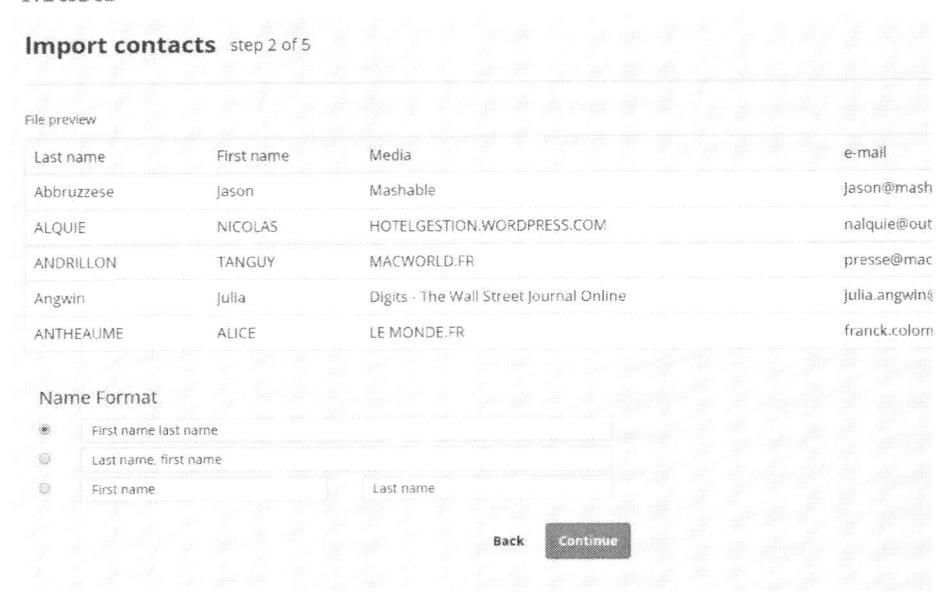

This is a powerful customer relationship management tool for bloggers, journalists, and works as a discovery platform. Within each tagged categories, you can choose journalists and bloggers for a specific niche. It is a great platform for brands that are on a budget, and it also caters to the objectives of large corporations.

Onalytica

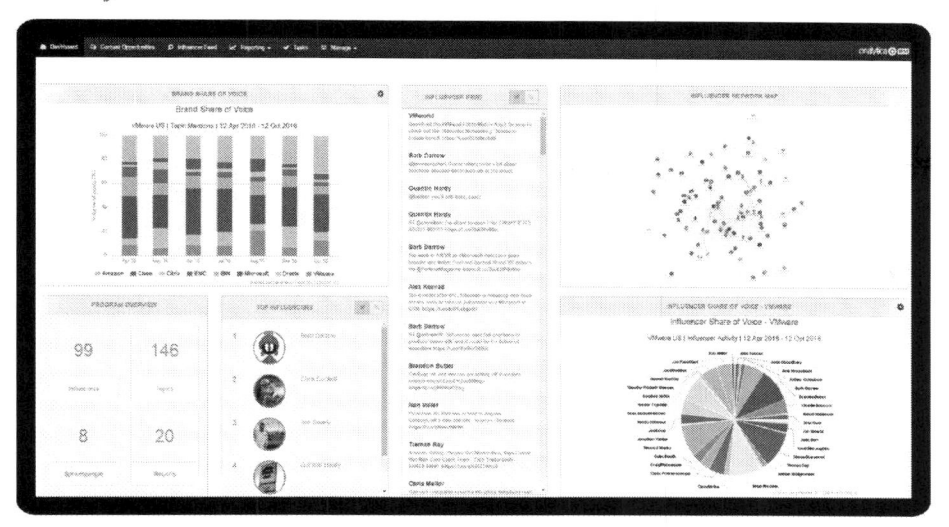

Onalytica combines algorithms and human oversight to filter the influencers in its database. It offers more than just influencer discovery. The platform also grants you the opportunity to listen, engage, measure, and scale your influencer marketing campaigns. Onalytica works for hiring influencers across popular platforms like Instagram, Twitter, LinkedIn, Facebook, and blogs.

Webfluential

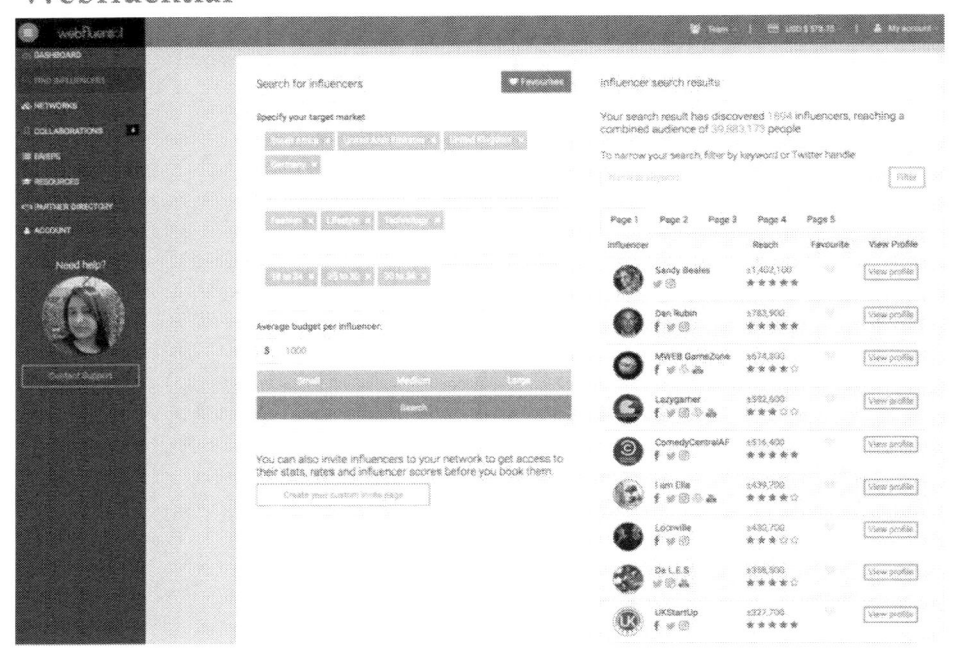

Webfluential stands out from other influencer marketing platforms by placing its priority on the quality of social media influencers instead of building the number of influencers on its platform. You can get access to the best influencers on Instagram, YouTube, Twitter, Facebook, and WordPress who have been vetted.

It is a great platform for small businesses and startups and even has an impressive clientele list that includes Coca-Cola. Subscription to a premium service on a monthly basis starts at $100 per month.

MARKETING YOURSELF AS AN INTROVERTED INFLUENCER

Introverts get a bad rap in the online world as people see them as the opposites of normal behavior. Introvert vs. Extrovert is always viewed as bad vs. good. However, I think of the two personalities differently. Being an introvert or extrovert depends on where you get your energy. Extroverts can be likened to a solar panel who suck energy from the surrounding and people around them. Introverts, on the other hand, are like an internal battery that attach to themselves to recharge.

What Do These Personalities Translate To Online

On the one hand, social media platforms serve as a solid way to interact with other people because you do not have to be with them physically – you can connect with thousands of people from the comfort of your room. However, this goes both ways.

The comfort of your room is no longer a haven from other people, and they're right with you wherever you go in your phone. There is zero room for an escape to charge your "online" battery, which is exhausting.

Social media frowns on introversion. It is tailored to bring out the outspoken side of your personality, with comments on posts and likes that roll out of your fingers like toilet top in high school movies. Social media does not have time for people who require constant personal space and time.

Don't get me wrong, however, even as an introvert, one of my favorite things to do is read and return comments from my followers, catching up on the latest trends and trying to sell my brand on multiple platforms. It just gets exhausting sometimes.

Thinking of original ways to connect with people that won't make me seem edgy or generally writes tends to drain the life force out of me. Before I decided to become an Instagram influencer, I was not used to connecting with new people, hell it never even occurred to me to say hi to new people online. It used to take an incredibly beautiful picture of a popular Instagrammer to get me to say hi.

Just like real life, I am not one to put myself out there. I only talk to my friends and respond only to people who approach me. Here's the bombshell. As an influencer, I will definitely tank. My dream of being an influencer is because I want to help brands sell on their industries. So, I decided to learn how to deal with my introverted nature, and get over my constant aversion to interaction.

I love people, but it is just hard to interact. If you are an aspiring influencer and in the same shoes, this section will help you learn how to succeed as a social media personality.

How To Succeed As An Introverted Influencer

Being a success on different social media platforms, especially Instagram requires you to deal with your introversion issues. I'm hoping the tips I lay out in this book help you to launch a successful influencer career, and adapt them for general life balance.

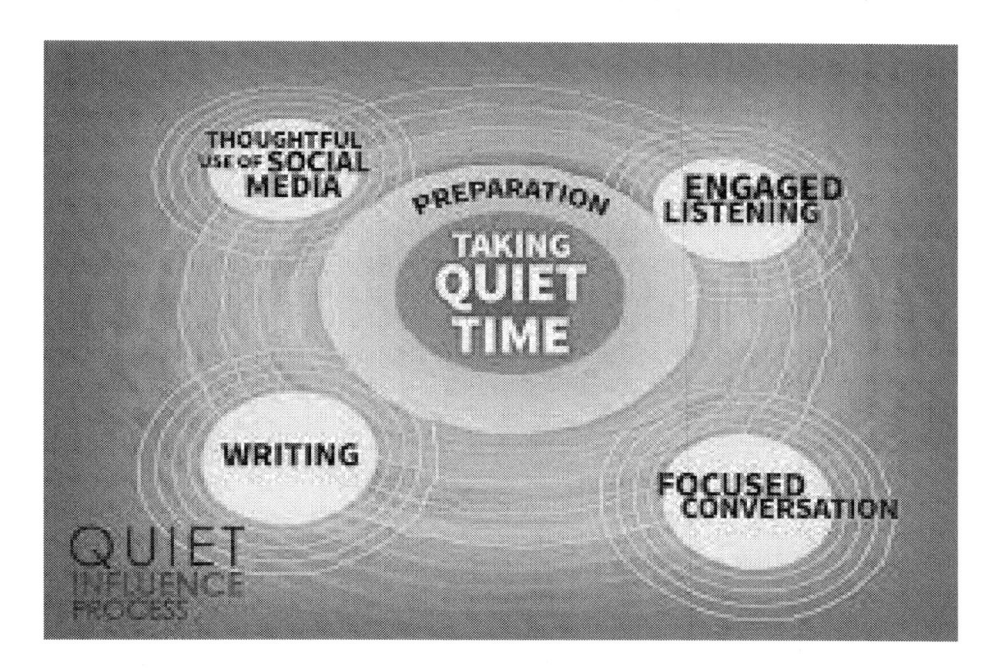

Source: Cooler Insights

Create A Routine

I have a list of things I regularly involve myself in to combat my introverted tendencies. When you develop a habit, it gets easier every passing day. Repeating an action every day like commenting leads to commenting momentum, and the more you practice, the better you get. A routine also gives you boundaries. If I calculate my engagement rate and see it is between 5 and 7, I can make a mental note of those hours and work on being productive during that time safe in the knowledge that I can put my phone down after to recharge my batteries.

If you are constantly working on your engagement without a set time, it becomes a daunting task that will increase your stress levels. Set a time for engagement and stick to it.

Engage at Your Highest

Earlier I mentioned that introverts run on what I call the internal battery. I have noted the sort of the things that usually drain it and what boost it, so when I am returning comments and interacting with followers, I make sure that I perform those actions in an area where I'm recharging my batteries. This can be on the sofa watching TV, at a pedicure salon, in bed on a weekend morning, or in a bubble bath.

This sense of relaxation fills me with good energy that I can translate to my online interactions. On the flip side, I avoid social media interactions when I am expending energy in real life – in between shuttles or on a train.

Challenge Yourself

I am very good at pushing myself, so a challenge brings out the best in me. There are different challenges I set for myself on a weekly basis, which often includes commenting on five of my followers, or doing a live Instagram story instead of scheduled posts. Sometimes it can be using five hashtags a week. This not only motivates me but it also gives me a sense of accomplishment. You can do it too, and your followers will appreciate the interaction and different posts. This leads me to the final part.

Reciprocating Energy

It feels awesome to receive a nice comment; hence you should change your mindset about online interactions from "uhhhhhh, dealing with people" to "I am going to compliment five people today." I realized early that it was selfish and a tad hypocritical to expect people to interact with me first when I was not willing to afford them the same courtesy.

A new person commenting or tagging you to appreciate your posts and Instagram feed hits different, so spread the love and appreciate your followers more. They are bound to feel obliged to do the same so suck it up and share the love!

The success of your career depends solely on you. Whether you are an Instagram influencer, a brand manager or an employee, you need to sell yourself. And the way part is you do not need money to start this process. Focus on marketing yourself and building an online presence through your social media profile so that you can scale to the next level. I have listed five

Effective ways to market yourself as an introverted influencer:

- **Write:** One for the quickest and most effective methods of promoting your online presence is to write and share content publicly. You can build credibility with a post on LinkedIn or by submitting articles to newspaper and online platforms. Market yourself and make yourself searchable on the interwebs.

- **Get Quoted:** Journalists and writers take pride in quoting expert opinions to bolster their argument. Be the expert in this scenario. Getting quoted by another individual increases your exposure to a different audience and promotes your impact in that niche. To become a force to be acknowledged on a particular topic, you must showcase your expertise. This can be done through your writing and professional experience. Journalists find individuals by searching for topics and pinpointing individuals who are experts in the subject.

- **Leverage Email**: Market yourself and your success via email. Share your writing. Make sure you include a link to any recently published article of yours. Email is very effective and should be used to promote your impact in your niche.

- **Utilize Social Media:** Whether it is Instagram, LinkedIn, Twitter, Facebook, or other social media platforms, demonstrate your impact on these sites. Sharing content on social media platforms affords you the opportunity to access a wider audience compared to direct email campaigns. A move like this can boost your brand exposure exponentially. Share links to articles and writeup where you have been quoted. Conduct reviews of news stores relevant to your niche and make an effort to be discovered on the Internet.

- **Speak Publicly**: While I understand this can be very hard for an introvert, public events can be a tough choice to promote yourself. However, they present decent opportunities to share your expertise and thoughts on topics trending in the industry. You don't have to appear live, as you can easily record a video or appear on a guest panel with other people to make it easier.

As an influencer, you may want to speak at an event sponsored by the Influencer Marketing Association. Speaking at an event like this opens you to opportunities where audience members can bid for your services. Regardless of where you work and what you do, it is important to identify speaking opportunities that provide you with a platform to market yourself and showcase what you and your brand offer.

Your career is your business. Focus on discovering easy, cost-efficient ways to promote your name on the Internet to create big opportunities for your yourself.

Promoting Your Brand As An Introvert

Jeremy Walter, the Head of Digital Strategy at **ExactTarget** once said something profile along the lines of "If there was ever a group of people who benefited from social media, it was shy people."

If you're shy and you have a service you want to sell it is very likely that you are in need of a wider audience. It is important to not compromise your standards and personality because of sales. The art of "pimping" yourself is a trait that buyers find unappealing. What you want is for your product to sell better without having to learn your standards with a shameless promotion that overrides your followers feed.

It is important to rise in the ranks without losing the trust of your followers if you are known as an influencer that prioritizes sales over customer relationship.

Shy vs. Introvert

There is a slight difference between shyness and introversion. It is commonplace for both elements to be grouped, but research has shown there is a notable difference between the two qualities. Shyness is learned behavior resulting from anxiety and discomfort m. Introversion, on the other hand, is a human trait that requires the individual to constantly get some quiet time where they can recharge their batteries before engaging in human interaction.

Introversion does not affect your chances of success or ability to build a successful brand. Research conducted by ISA Today shows that an average of four in ten company executives are introverts. A notable example mentioned by Susan Cain in her blog, **Psychology Today,** is billionaire Bill Gates who is an introvert but not shy.

He is a quiet and bookish man who does not seem interested in others opinion of his lifestyle. He regularly attends seminars where he delivers a speech and most his time in the limelight is restricted to compulsory events like his foundation and product launches. As n introvert, he is not a fan of human interaction and reports claim he bought about eight houses surrounding his home to avoid disturbance and irregular activity.

Dorie Clark, A reputable marketing strategy consultant and a frequent contributor to Forbes and Harvard Business Review says "As an introvert, I have learned to play to my strengths while building my brand."

Shyness, by all accounts, is a barrier to your success as an individual. It stops people from being decisive when it comes to steps that can contribute to the success of their brand. Shyness fuels the fear of failure. And because of that, as a shy influencer, it is very easy to doubt the content you want to promote.

If the content you promote is beneficial to your audience, there several techniques that can help you overcome shyness while building a reputable personal brand at the same time.

You can be shy and still achieve your goals. As long as you strive your success coupled with creative ideas, you are on the right path. In 2019, everyone is a media outlet thanks to the internet. Nowadays, personal branding is the go-to for entrepreneurs that operate on the Internet, with plenty of opportunities for individuals to create their brand across several industries.

I believe that companies should provide support to shy personnel as a means to aid their branding ambitions by inserting bylaws into the HR policy.

A good personal brand is a representative of who you are. This is why it is essential to present yourself in the best possible way. Ideally, a good personal brand is a brand that is trusted by the audience. Building an excellent personal brand will give you access to like-minded individuals who are on the same reasoning wavelength as you. Growing and managing your brand, if done right, is an exciting process.

And the most valuable metric to gauge the success of your brand is if you don't lose your integrity as a person by staying true to your core values.

Finding the Right Strategy

Your works best when you represent your brand's ideal, and there are similarities in your lifestyle and your brand's message. Your brand must be an extension of your self. Ideally, your brand is expected to be an expression of your personality. A good brand is supposed to the best version of yourself. By clarifying what causes your shyness, there are ways to break down the hold it has over your work.

However, there is excellent news. Through platforms like social media, forums, and blogs you can avoid interactions that make you uncomfortable and achieve your goals of building your brand at the same time.

Taking note of the specific components of your introversion/Shyness is the first step in your branding journey. For example, if the underlying cause of your shyness is your appearance, it's best to stay away from video blogs and selfies. You should focus on creating and curating content.

Understanding Yourself

What are you shy about? Ask yourself that question. Usually, every shy person has a specific reason for their discomfort. Is it your voice? Eye contact? Appearance? Your failures? Fear of the unknown? Colleagues? Family? Strangers? Your aspirations? Your successes? Your values? Other reasons?

After identifying the reason behind your shy nature, the second leg of your branding journey begins. In this aspect, You need to focus on identifying the places and things that you aren't shy around. Is it your friends? Family? Do you engage in conversations when it comes to sports? Colleagues? Partners? Team? Hobby? Others?

This way you can choose a starting point for your brand. By identifying your areas of comfort, you can choose the niche you are most comfortable to start your online craft as an influencer. One of the most effective first steps – especially for any and introverted individuals – is to affirm your social presence by liking posts on Instagram. Liking posts on platforms like Instagram and Facebook is a fabulous way to get noticed especially when done periodically. If you so desire, you can even start an influencer marketing blog with other influencers in your niche to discuss your passion. Alternatively, you can restrict the blog to a closed membership before going mainstream.

Selling Your Brand Without Selling

Nite that social media marketing is the focus here because I have had the majority of inquiries from influencers and brands who want to sell their products and boost their exposure as an entity through social media platforms but are unable to.

Most of the inquiries always revolve around the same questions "how do I pass my message across to my audience," "I put up sponsored post, but I don't receive any returns on behalf of my clients." The cause of your poor feedback or sales is that you have not given your audience a reason to want your product.

I have a notable real-life example of this type of scenario. Let's say we are having a conversation for the first time and I keep talking about myself and what I can offer you throughout the conversation without asking about your concerns. Would you be interested in booking a follow-up conversation with me? Suffice to say, the answer is more than likely to be a big NO.

Relation and Education

You need to give your followers aplenty of reasons to like you. Social marketing – and other forms of marketing – requires that you focus less on your brand and more on your customers. Even though it sounds counter-intuitive, getting to know the concerns of your audience and discussing these issue gives you a chance to educate them about topics you are an expert in. When the audience feel like their concerns are being taken under consideration, they will be receptive to your solution

Remember, you are an expert, and your audience will respect your opinion. But only if they trust that you have their best interests in mind. Showcase your expertise and work on building healthy customer relationships. For example, if you are in the hair product niche, offer daily tips on how to choose the best hair products. Provide links to video tutorials that explain everything your audience is interested in.

When you eventually offer them products, it will be a no-brainer to purchase the product and services.

Showcasing your technical know-how of topics will make the consumers appreciate your contributions to their Instagram feed. The next time they think of a hair product or watch a tutorial, you will be on their minds. This is how you can market your services without flooding your feed with generic sponsored posts.

Allow The Audience To Express Themselves

Let your audience talk about themselves. Everyone desires to be noticed and feel important. Tap into that need for expression. Create a poll and ask questions that are related to your brand and give room for the audience to participate. One of the more impressive points about this strategy is that it increases engagement and also afford you the chance to know what your audience wants.

Without realizing it, the audience is revealing their interests and learning at the same time.

Let's use the hair product example again. It can be a good idea to ask hour followers "what recommended hair products do you get from friends that did not work for you?" Questions like this give your audience the opportunity to interact and participate with your account, AND it helps you identify the struggles your customers are dealing with.

Equipped with this knowledge, you can create a workshop or use the Instagram story feature to share useful hair product tips and offer services from the brand you are collaborating with.

Sense of Humor Is Vital

The ability to make your audience laugh is vital to possess as an influencer. Your posts do not have to revolve around giveaways and sponsored posts. Don't be afraid to post content that is unrelated to the brand you're working with.

Again, the hair product example works well here. You can post a picture of your pet having a bad hair day with a caption that reads "Looks like Jan needs an awesome hair product." You can start from the topic but be sure to link back to the audience.

Use the 80/20 Rule

Contrary to popular myths, it is good to promote yourself. By creating a fun relationship with your followers and ensuring that 80% of your content is aimed at the audience, you can promote your account 20% of the time without the fear of losing their interest.

After you have successfully provided valuable content to your audience, interacted with them, and allowed them to express their views, they will be willing to learn about your promotions without feeling your page just another typical salesy influencer account.

There are different ways to sell your brand's product without posting generic content along the lines of "Limited edition hair shampoo…buy it now!" Refrain from using "buy it now." That particular pitch does not resonate well with customers. Instead, be creative and upload the picture of the product with a simple caption that reads " It's waiting for you!"

Salesman Era Is Over

Sure, you're not a salesman. Luck you, people don't want to be sold to. You can skin your content in different ways without outright selling your product and service to your followers. This is the most effective way to build engagement and customer relationship.

Remember, if you go through your feed and realize that more than 20% of your posts focus on your brand, it is time to switch things up and change your strategy. Tone down the self-centered posts and focus on interacting with your customers. That is how to sell without selling.

If this section has helped you deal with your introverted nature as an influencer, you can help other readers browsing through Amazon to read this book by dropping 5 star feedback on our page. Thank you.

HOW BRANDS AND INFLUENCERS CAN MAKE MONEY TOGETHER

Various brands have failed with influencer marketing within the past few years, with multiple brands also succeeding in the process. A common factor within the failed brands is that they don't have a suitable relationship with their influencers.

All they want is to make money through their influencers, and they have failed to see the reason why they should also make money for their influencers. Most of them think paying them is enough. This is correct in some cases, but then, most of these relationships are short-lived.

If you want to benefit from influencer marketing in the long run actively, you also need to help your influencers in benefiting more from your partnership. This will help both you and them at the same time.

Check out the new influencer program Amazon just launched, the program is very lucrative for influencers because it provides them with a customized page that allows them to compliment all product recommendation of theirs.

It purposefully combats the problems related with affiliate links that can't be clickable on video content and Instagram photo captions. They made it easier for audiences to move from the discovery page to a conversation page.

This is a simple example of influencers and brands working together for mutual benefits. Here are some simple ways in which brands and influencers can help them self-make money.

1. Networking

This is an easy and effective way used by influencers and brands to benefit from networking mutually. A brand can help promote its influencers at different PR events like press conferences. This will help to enhance your influencer connections and visibility.

It will also foster a better relationship between you and the influencer which will naturally increase his interest in promoting your brand.

2. Content Sharing

Big brands usually have a broader reach when it comes to non-celebrity influencers. Your influencers become more visible when you share their contents on your social channels. This will help them gain more followers and sometimes partnership with other brands.

You probably think what's in it for you as a brand, for one, if you share readymade content, it will boost your content sharing strategy. Also, since these contents are made by your trusted influencers, you have high-quality and creative content in your hands.

This will help you gain audience engagement and simultaneously increase your customers' trust. Therefore, I recommend brands to share their trusted influencers' content on their social media channels.

4. Partnerships

As a brand, you can easily partner with different influencers for an extended campaign. The important benefit from this endorsement is an increase in brand awareness. Alternatively, it also helps to improve the brands' image of your influencer so more collaborations can be landed.

Here is an excellent example of how partnerships can easily benefit influencers and brands

Airbnb partnered with a famous travel blogger known as Jack Morris for a series of posts on his social media channels. Throughout all his campaign, his travel and stay were sponsored by Airbnb. This helped to boost brand awareness for both the brand as well as the influencer.

5. Free Product Samples

Brands should share free samples of their products with their influencers. This will help foster a good relationship with the influencer and with time, encourage them to use your products.

As an influencer, you have to share your recommendations and reviews on your social media channels. You can easily combine your recommendations with an affiliate link or a discount code from the brand. When your followers make a purchase, you and your company can easily make mutual gains from it.

Let's take Jacob True as an example. He is an influencer in the photography and travel niche, which he often shares on Instagram. In one of his posts, he conjoined with an apparel brand known as UNTUCKit. He wore one of their shirts and included an affiliate link in his bio.

> **jacobtrue** • Follow
>
> **jacobtrue** Stoked to be collaborating with UNTUCKit - The shirts designed to be worn untucked. For every sale made through the link in my bio, UNTUCKit will donate $8 to charity! #linkinbio @UNTUCKit #UNTUCKit #ad
>
> **oliviarackley** Aw!
>
> **davesarazen** So handsome I could die 😍
>
> **reneedufour** @alexisreneebell I thought this pic could help your studying😊
>
> **alexisreneebell** @reneedufour 😍😍 now that's just distracting...... so cruel
>
> **jasontuno** SLAY
>
> **reneedufour** @alexisreneebell hahaha you're welcome
>
> **realpalermini** My dawg
>
> **faith_uphoff** Looking great!!!!
>
> ♡ 💬
>
> 1,057 likes
>
> 3 DAYS AGO

However, influencers must include their association with specific brands explicitly. It is a mandate but the Federal Trade Commission, and it is also a good practice. On any endorsement or production, you should mention your compensation (nonmonetary or momentary).

With at least 600 million audience and active users, there's a 100 percent chance that your target customers are on Instagram. You can quickly get them engaged in your post by creating thoughtful and imaginative contents. Some nifty strategies are also required to help it spread wide and far.

The relationship between influencers and brands can't be a one-way street. If there's no mutual benefit, the relationship can collapse easily. Therefore, use the tip above to improve your relationship with your influencer to gain long-term benefits.

With just a sponsored and billions of snaps, Instagram is now one of the most popular photo-sharing apps. Even though it is not straight forward to marketers, most brands owners know Instagram is not just about puppy videos and selfies.

These are nine examples of brands that explicitly used Instagram marketing.

1. National Geographic

With Instagram, the best contents have a way of getting found. You can confirm this with National Geographic. With just 74.2 million followers, most of their materials are very popular. No memes. No gimmicks. Just amazing pictures of seals that capture the imagination.

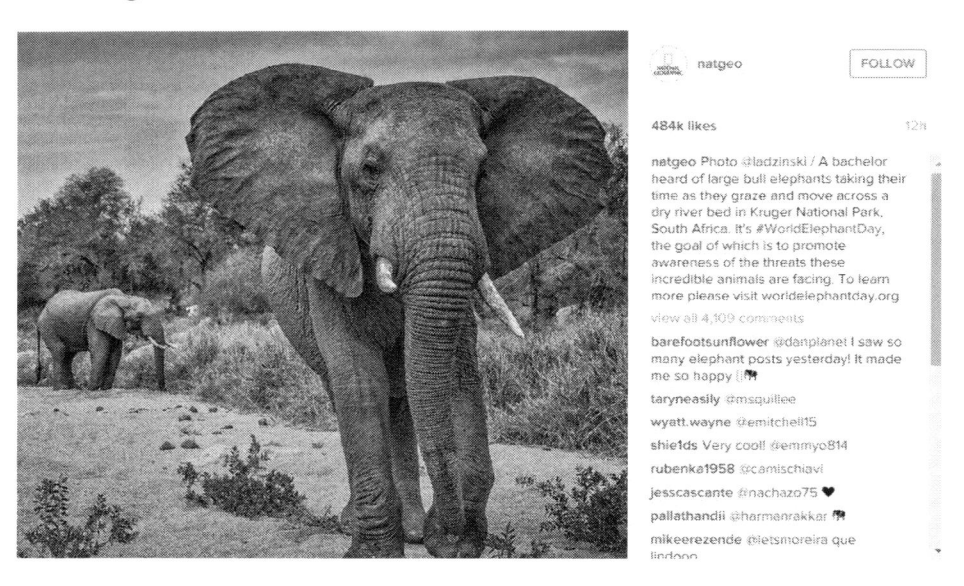

This has also given National Geographic an army of professional photographers that spend their lives exploring the globe. It is an excellent example of doing one thing and doing it awesomely. Get snapping and zero in your niche.

2. Adidas Neo

One of the ways brands market their products is by spending millions of dollars on ad placements. This is another easy way to allow your audience to do the work for you.

Adidas created a campaign to promote their Neo Brand, and the campaign asked their followers to create an Instagram post with the hashtag #MyNeoShoot. The best contents were then used to model in a professional photo shoot, and the result was then rolled out on the Adidas Instagram channel. Adidas also enlisted the support of some favorite celebrity like Selena Gomez to help spread the word about the content.

Adidas generated up to 71, 000 mentions of the hashtag #MyNeoShoot and also gained up to 41,000 followers. This is a perfect example that should help that creative content will help engage your audience and also boasts the power of social media influencers.

3. Bloom & Wild

You don't need to waste money on different campaigns before securing excellent results on Instagram. Bloom & Wild is a luminous example of how to grow a business with Instagram ads without big-brand budgets.

The delivery startup is aimed at attracting a broader audience to their fledgling business. They, therefore, turned to Instagram. To make most of their budget, they used the existing email list to target their lookalike audience on Instagram through the Facebook Power Editor. After different tests were made, they found out that Video ads make their best conversion rate, and thus doubled down on their efforts.

Bloom & Wild also increase their bouquet order to 62% and realized a considerable upswing in their new customers' comments on their Instagram profile. It is also a classic example of how staying on top of your metrics can help provide the best out of a limited budget.

4. Bejeweled

Social media influencers are usually quite powerful on Instagram. This was the case for the developers of the gaming app **Bejeweled**, who partnered with Instagram influencers to inside millions to purchase the app.

Bejeweled used a campaign with a creative YouTube short that features people - and pupils influencer Jiffpom – using the game as a liberator from boredom.

The campaign also used top Instagram influencers like Kola Webb and David Lopez who helped by sharing the video of them playing the game with the specific hashtag #shinyplace. These influencers use their followers to the same, and you know - the rest is history.

With just a month after the campaign launched, the game climbed from 702 to 182 in the chart of top grossing US App store apps. This confirmed the fact that, if you CNN pay influencers to promote your service and product, you'll get results.

5. Old Spice Dream Runner

This brand has a reputation for its whimsical, witty ad campaign. Also, reputation can sometimes cause more harm than good. How does Old Spice keep topping the vanguard of edgy advertising? How do you engage in marketing collateral when your audience already had a clear expectation for your creativity? The answer to these questions for Old Spice was to pull maximum efforts into the unfamiliar territory of social media.

This was how the Dream Runner Campaign was orchestrated.

> loganpaul ✓ • Follow
>
> loganpaul MAKING SHAPES OUT OF YOUR RUN! 🏃‍♂️ Get your workout on with oldspicedreamrunner.com & their Hardest Working Collection. Run your own shape! @oldspice will be awarding awesome prizes #runoldspice #ad
>
> Load more comments
>
> angel.andreeva Мне послышалось порно 😂😂😂
>
> beatles4lif That last second reminded me of jack black
>
> lilmisa210 Trying to get your attention I sent a dm
>
> starr.madsen That's hilarious
>
> fatemeh____16 😍
>
> destiny_bug My best friend loves you!!!!!!
>
> ♡ ○   ☐
>
> 3,283,124 views
>
> MAY 13, 2016
>
> Add a comment...   ...

Runners never had it so good. There are various apps available for you to track your runs and also highlight the pats you followed as you move across your area. You can even share the routes you conquered through social media. This is the precise technology that the Old Spice requires to piggyback on.

The Dream Runner campaign tells their followers to win different kinds of stuff by posting different photos of a running route in a similar shape of the price tell wanted – with the hashtag #runoldspice. The campaign tagline was "If you can run it, you can own it."

Influential Instagrammers played an essential role in this campaign by helping the Old Spice reach their campaign goals; promote the Hardest Working Collection and enhancing identity as an innovative brand.

Old Spice invited some famous personalities like Kevin LeSean (fitness devotee and musician), Shalvis (parkour specialist), and Logan Paul (entertainer) to engage in the campaign. These choices were not random and were exceptionally clever. These personalities were popular with the target demographic and were also big on fitness and health. Also, Logan Paul is especially humorous.

This is a good example that shows how to reduce market friction by selecting influencers that match your brand values and can promote the product in a way that will be adored by most of the people exposed to the campaign.

6. Chanel

One of the simplest ways to reach your target market is to move to people that can. This is why Chanel invited a series of the world's top beauty and fashion bloggers to the south of France for a free retreat.

This was synonymous to the time when Chanel wanted to launch their No. 5 L'Eau perfume. The gathering that took place in the South of France was also a get together for the fashion blogging community. Chanel masterstroke was to give the bloggers invited a tour of their facilities in the town of Grasse. Chanel also allows the blogger to explore the flower fields and explained how they made their fragrance from real flowers.

They also encouraged their bloggers to document their exploration on Instagram with the hashtags #chanelgrasse and #newchanel5. This helped one of the best perfume producers to create some unbelievable results. The hashtag #newchanel5 attracted over 900,00 likes in their first month of the campaign while the hashtag #newchanel5 generated over 1,600 individual contents (both influencers and users that uploaded their images).

Chanel's strategy of directly moving to their target audience's beauty and fashion heroes exposed them to up to 9 million followers with social media. Although, this is more than reach. The campaign also taps into the customer's desire to be behind the curtain. To see things behind the scenes.

Can your brand do something similar?

7. Sonic Drive-In

If you can compare Instagram with any shape, it'll be the square. The Sonic Drive-In was keen to tap into that with their geometrically pleasing milkshakes.

Here are the highlights of the campaign. The square milkshakes were created by a culinary Instagram merely known as Chef Jacques LeMerde – and they were sold during the Coachella Music and Arts Festival. They have shop-on-demand integrations that allowed customers room chose between flavors through an ad on Instagram and had their milkshake delivered hand-to-hand (clever use of geo-fencing) and paid for their

125

frothy beverage, frigid by merely making a post with the hashtag #SquareShakes.

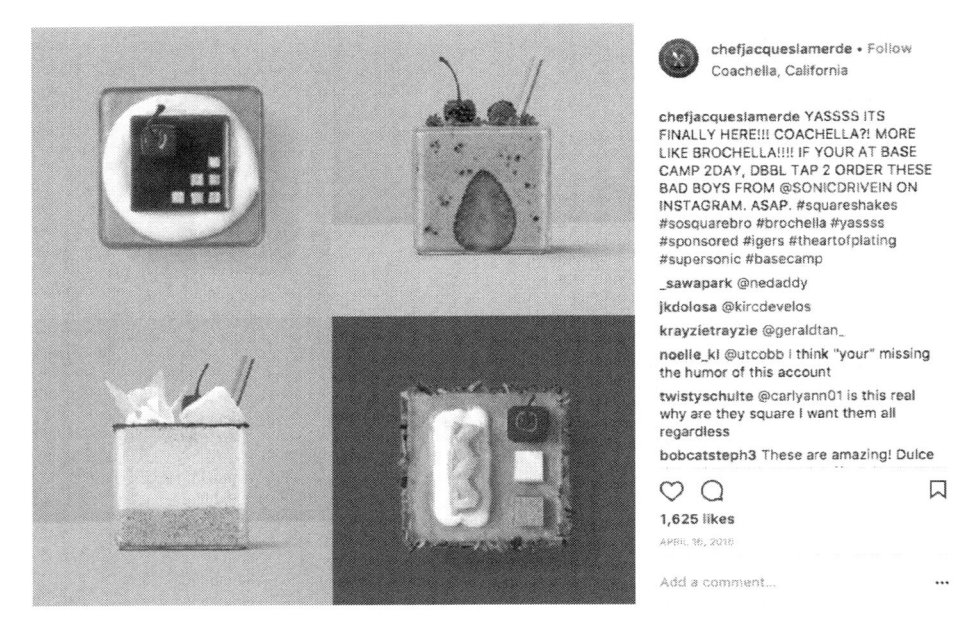

[Instagram post by chefjacqueslamerde from Coachella, California showing square milkshakes. Caption: "YASSSS ITS FINALLY HERE!!! COACHELLA?! MORE LIKE BROCHELLA!!!! IF YOUR AT BASE CAMP 2DAY, DBBL TAP 2 ORDER THESE BAD BOYS FROM @SONICDRIVEIN ON INSTAGRAM. ASAP. #squareshakes #sosquarebro #brochella #yassss #sponsored #igers #theartofplating #supersonic #basecamp". 1,625 likes, APRIL 16, 2016.]

The campaign generated up to 1000 comments and increased Sonic's follower count from 118,000 to 129,000. This is yet another example of Instagram being a vehicle for a more time-honored marketing strategy. Sonic utilized one of the old tricks in the book to raise awareness of their desserts - giving them for free.

Using traditional marketing strategies with digital in a creative way can help get you the results you want.

8. Airbnb

The best campaign ideas pass through the pores of your entire marketing collateral, copy, images, and tone of voice. The best idea can inform a lot – no matter the channel you work with. Unfortunately, brands often think that coming up with some snappy tagline will do the job. Airbnb is not the type.

Airbnb orchestrated a campaign tagline 'don't just go there, live there' which sounds like a call to arms. They backed up the idea by posting user-generated photos from both guests and hosts. The campaign gave users something interesting to engage in. And it also earned Airbnb thousands of likes per post.

The campaign is an excellent example of being real. It shows the importance of making sure a campaign Idea shows the identity of your brand and explains your marketing output.

9. Hartley's 10 Cal Jelly

Hartley wants to raise awareness of their 10 Cal jelly among British females between 25 and 34. There's no better time than January when the fitness and health resolutions are still fresh in mind.

The social media campaign – incorporated Instagram, Facebook, and Twitter – and was based on the tagline "Are you a #Dietdevil or a #10CalAngel?" The brand sent up to 10 Cal jelly to the power middle of Instagram diet influencers (the ones with up to 10,000 followers), Hartley got some fantastic results.

Over a hundred Instagram followers engaged with the campaign and posted up to 295 times to their followers. That increased Hartley engagement rate by 146% and also double their followers can't. And most importantly, their sales increased by a lot. Over to you.

Instagram marketing can sometimes be a pain in the ass. But – as it shows in the examples above – it is far from impossible. Instagram is a physical, visual media. Make sure you present your brand visually. Create ways of rewarding people and utilize user-generated content for posting photos that will promote your brand.

Use Instagram as a way to offer freebies. Tap into the persuasive resources of influencers to link up with your target customers. You don't even have to act salesy, and you have to know your brand. And of course, a little creativity will go a very long way.

Bearing n mind that you have learnt a lot about Instagram and influencer marketing practices, kindly drop a 5 star feedback on our Amazon page to help other readers tap into theis rich book that explores everything you need to do to achieve a successful influencing career.

Creating The Best Instagram Captions As an Instagram Influencer

Source: GramLike

A good Instagram caption can break or make your Instagram marketing game. Think about it.

A well-crafted Instagram caption has three great importance:

- They allow you to add hashtags (thereby increasing your chances of getting new followers)
- They give you an opportunity to include a call-to-action (telling your followers how they should react to your posts);

- They let you show off your personality (giving you a chance to stand out as a brand);

Instagram captions are very crucial to your success on the platform. And yet, they are overlooked most times.

Truth is if you're the type that thinks "anything goes" when it comes to your caption on IG, it is time to change that mindset. Although these captions may not seem very important at a glance, they represent an essential piece of engagement he tween yourself and your followers.

If you think there's room to improve your Instagram caption game, don't hesitate to do it. Here are seven caption strategies that'll help your imprint your level of followers engagement. Regardless of the things you're trying to achieve, some combos of these tips will help you out.

1. Tell your story

The quote "A picture's worth a thousand words" could not be more right on Instagram. Every business and their photos tell a story, don't they?

Have a storytelling caption on your posts on Instagram makes business more 'real' with the followers. The captions have a humanizing effect that passes through your brand, giving you a voice and a face, when you tell stories.

Take a look at Canva to see what I mean.

They made a campaign about telling different personal stories of their customers, telling what their deal is, who they were, and how they use Canva. This aspect is more than just storytelling, and it also proves you need to engage with your followers on way or another.

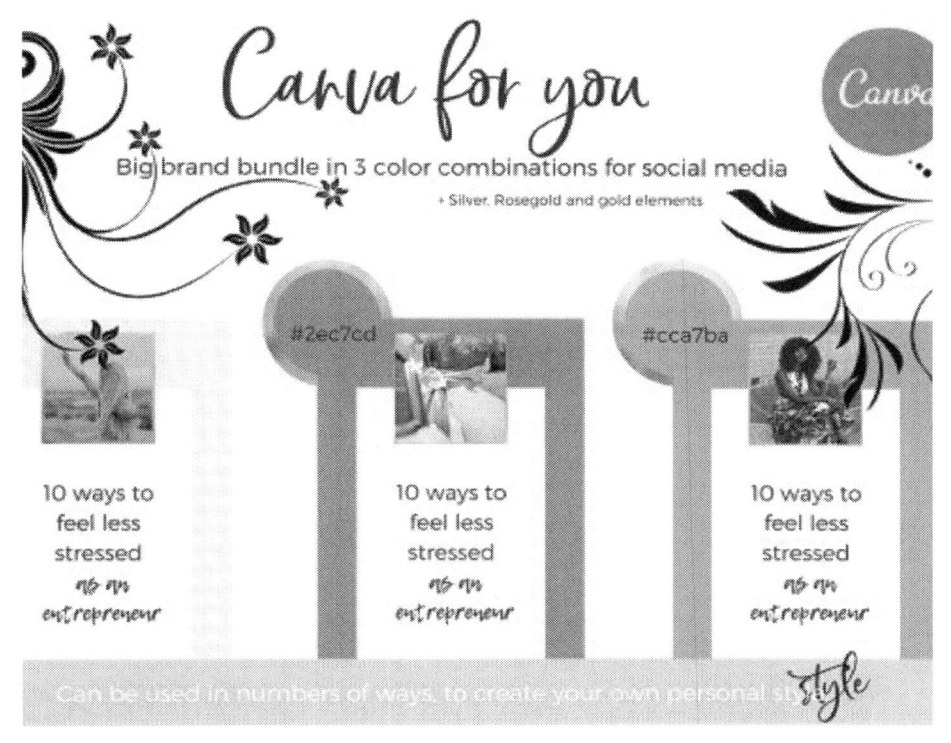

Storytelling in Captions is a crucial way to engage with your followers.

Just like humorous Captions, Storytelling posts aren't what brand implements daily. They are just an effective way to tweak your regular content to spice it up a bit. When met with a bulk of text that unusual, most followers tend to take notice.

This does not mean some brands don't thrive off Storytelling captions as regular content, though. Humans of New York is an explicit example of how different stories can tow the heartstrings of your followers:

Storytelling in Instagram captions

Just make sure there's a positive message at the core of the caption, and they must be related to your brand or business. You're set!

2. Don't be afraid to ask

If you want something, something the best way to get it is to ask.

If you feel that your followers have recently grown a bit cold, or you're strapped for Instagram captions, you should consider use information captions that indirectly or directly poses a question to your followers. This will reduce your chances of being tagged as over-promotional, and it can quickly help you learn more about your customers.

Question-based captions also serve as an opportunity to encourage comments and likes that sometimes would not receive that much engagement. Let us take Southwest Airlines as an example, and they sometimes ask some playful trivia-style questions to their followers:

A question at the end of a caption tends to increase the number of comments on a post, with people participating and chiming in on the thread.

An important tip: always remember that people like to talk about themselves. Therefore you should consider asking them something personal and straightforward like what they did yesterday? What are thy up to? What's their favorite color? There's a wide variety of things to ask actually. It's okay if you don't know where to start, keep in mind that asking something personal from your audience doesn't need a paragraph or a questionnaire to be effective. Sometimes, a simple "How was your day" can go a long way.

Starbucks perfected the question-based caption recently in an Instagram post where followers were asked to discuss their favorite region for coffee production.

Finally, question-based captions aren't meant for just engagement alone on your Instagram post. They also serve as a means for personal research, a way to learn something about your following, and subsequently increasing your Instagram strategy.

133

3. A sense of humor never hurt anybody

Personality usually means a lot for businesses looking to define a brand identity on Instagram.

Rather than using a consistent "suit and tie" approach on your content, you should consider spicing things up with some humor on your field. Your followers will appreciate it more than the usual salesy, spammy contents. Give your followers something to laugh about to define your brand and also stand out from the crowd.

Baby talks

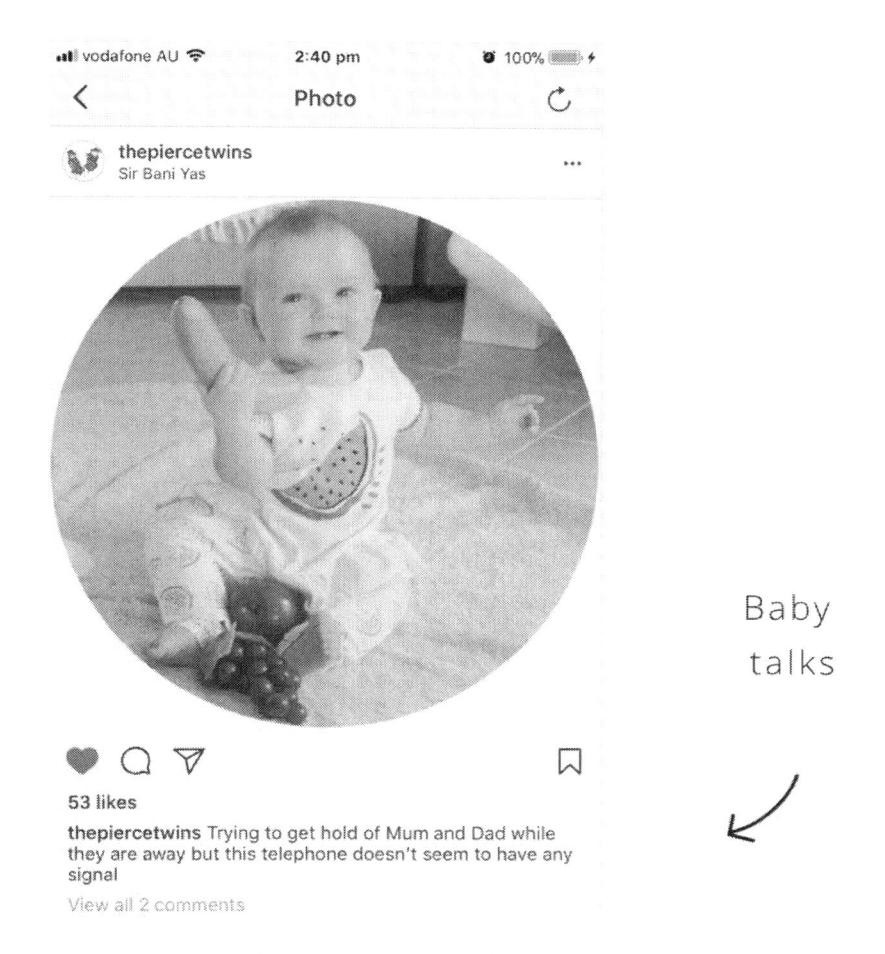

However, you don't need to be a constant comedian on Instagram, make light-hearted part now and then to provide a nice touch for your followers. Check out this hilarious post from Warby Parker as an example:

The post is sweet, easy to consume, and easy to engage with – the caption is also cute, short, and it also flows with the message.

4. Show your followers some love

In the modern world, user-generated contents are becoming more and more critical to Instagram, especially considering that

UGC helps to generate up to 6.9x higher engagement that the usual brand contents. If you're blessed with followers that like your content and are satisfied with your products, and they often sing your praises, you should mention them once a while in your caption to show some love.

Even big brands like Starbucks often take their time to engage their followers. (Make sure you do this accordingly, and always ask permission before using their contents as a part of your campaign.)

When it comes to terms of caption copy for UGC, a simple "thanks" usually suffice, sometimes it is a snappy one-liner with their customers' photos. However, you can even move further and tell a story about the user that had his post regrammed by you.

Either way, always consider a good caption for UGC posts to create a sense of appreciation for the followers that keep showing off your products to encourage others to do the same.

5. Hone in on your hashtags

Simple and plain, Instagram captions that feature hashtags usually brings about more engagement that the ones without them. Moreover, it takes a few minutes to add some hashtags to your post.

Choosing the right hashtags for your post should not be a tedious job. Businesses have a choice between non-branded and branded hashtags or a combo of both.

For example, some big brands usually engage with branded hashtags, not just to harvest UGC, but to also strengthen their brand story or an actual campaign.

However, sometimes the best choice is non-branded hashtags.

Although hashtags are usually used to increase the discoverability of a post or to boost an engagement rate, they also serve an essential role in narrative lyrics complementing your photo. That is, the hashtags do not necessarily need to be straightforward. They can also be personalized, funny, newly invented by you, or just an additional to an original caption.

Use hashtags in Instagram captions

Being different is okay. Just be creative!

6. Take advantage of tagging

A good Instagram caption will not just reward and show love to your usual followers, and it should also work to bring a new audience to your feed.

As a result, you can use the "tag a friend" caption as a playful way to encourage your followers to introduce non-followers and friends to your business. Tag-a-friend posts are often coupled with topical hashtags to give followers a chance to give a shoutout to someone.

A great example is a post by Alex Andani, who used the #BestFriendsDay hashtag to ask followers to tag their besties:

However, Tag-a-friend posts are not something businesses should use all the time, they're just an organic, fun way to engage your followers – and also a fresh idea for an Instagram caption.

7. Sometimes less is more

It is okay to let the picture speak for themselves sometimes.

Minimalist captions are the direct opposite of storytelling posts, and it is the process of using a few words to highlight a striking or bold image. There's no real secret to the act, and just like the storytelling posts, they should be used sparingly. Here are some effective yet simple samples from H&M.

Minimalist captions provide yet another stylish way to make an impression on followers. Take a look at how Forever21 uses just a 3-word caption to make an impression:

Also, if you're not feeling creative enough to craft a minimalist caption yourself, you could always use any one-liners from song lyrics or famous quotes if you're desperate for inspiration.

As you can see, regarding the process of crafting captions, there is no shortage of options for business on Instagram. From mainstays, such as UGC and hashtags, to slightly more creative options like storytelling, brands have a lot to do when it comes to making their posts stand out in the feeds.

When you schedule and plan your Instagram content. Pre-scheduled content ahead of time always helps.

The Best Time to Post on Instagram

A fundamental question that has kept thousands of Instagrammers awake at night. Choosing the premium hour to release content can be very difficult depending on your target audience, but that is why you are reading this book, yes? To make it easier, of course.

Well, it is quite a tough one. Identifying the best time to post on Instagram always helps to increase the engagement and reach of your posts, which is quite essential when it comes to the new Instagram algorithm.

There are various articles out there that bits of advice on the best time to post on Instagram. Some might tell you to do it on Thursday by 4 pm. Other might say you should avoid post at that time because of one reason or another.

Then there are others that will swear that you'll get the best engagement when you post by 12-1pm. I know. Confusing.

The thing is, there's no general solution to this problem. This is because the best time to post on Instagram depends entirely on your person. That is, it depends on you, your brand, and your target audience, which is usually different from each other.

Qualitative research is required to find the optimum posting time. Also, ironically, it also needs time.

When is the best time to put up posts on Instagram?

First of all, why does it matter to post at a particular time on your Instagram?

Good question.

Releasing posts at the right time will help you gain more audience, which would inevitably result in higher engagement rates. It is vital to drive most of your attention to your post in the first 15-20 minutes, and this is because the algorithm favors posts that get an initial spike of likes. Once your post attracts a lot of engagement immediately after it is posted, the algorithms immediately tell Instagram your content has excellent quality – and that the algorithm should make it more visible for more people to see.

Various engagement techniques are available to gather the first like. For example, commenting on others content right after you posted yours, boosting your content through ads, using targeted hashtags, and more.

However, all your work could be in vain if you make a post when your existing audience is not online. You won't generate the first likes, which are very important for engagement if you post your contents at a period when your audience is not online to see it.

Which takes us to the first step of your research: Finding out wen your Instagram followers are online!

When are your followers online on Instagram?

The quicker the engagement, the higher the lifetime value of your posts. That is, if you're lucky to post at a time where most of your followers are only, you're giving your contents the opportunity to be seen and liked!

Make a post at the "peak online" is synonymous to hacking the Instagram algorithm

So how do you know when your followers are online?

Simple, Ask Instagram!

Go to Insights → Audience and scroll a little down, and you'll see on the actual days of the week — and the approximate times — your followers are the most active on Instagram.

This data will provide a good understanding of the best time to make a post, based on your type of audience.

Where to track your Instagram followers online

If you're looking for the exact hour-by-hour breakdown, you can also look at the Iconosquare in the Analytics then the Reach section. The most colored boxes show the hour which most of your followers are online, while the least colored spaces show the opposite:

When are my Instagram followers online?

This is quite simple: Choose the hours when most of your followers will come online, then make your posts to coincide with such hours.

Experiment with posting times

As a marketer, experimenting and testing should be your mantra, especially on social media. When you've established the stipulated time that your audience is most likely to be online, the next thing is to used different posting time as an experiment to identify the best Optimal Hour.

Select a particular period when your followers are likely to be most active and post any different times within that period, to track their engagement rates.

For example, if you have noticed that majority of your followers are mostly only between 5 pm to 9 pm, you should schedule your posts to appear at 1, 2, 3, 4, 5, and 6 pm. Also, if you'd like to do the tracking normally, notice the engagement rate of these posts, along with the time and day of publishing.

Change the timing of your posts every week. If you publish at 1 pm this Friday, you can try to release at 1 am instead the next time. After you have all the data you need to overview, highlight the time slots with the best engagement rates:

What does Instagram analytics tell you?

If you're not a fan of spreadsheets, you can also rely on analytics to determine the beat times to post on Instagram.

After you've published various contents, analytics will help you compare your posting habits and your successful contents to determine if you're posting at the right time.

When it comes to picking your optimal posting times, though, don't forget that the quality of your contents is also quite relevant here. Different content types get different engagement rates, and this is why it's always to post different media on the same day today at the same hour of the week. With this, you'll be able to accumulate more engagement on every slot, which will be super useful for Iconosquare when making suggestions based on your posts.

Best time to post on Instagram

You can filter your results easily by likes, comments, and engagement, and then chose a data range on our date picker.

The black circles display on the perimeters show the days and hours that you often post.

The best of times are usually stared.

The blue-colored circles show your premium posting times while the smaller blue circles represent less optimal, but also active times to post.

Sometimes, it could take up to a few weeks for the data to accumulate, be patient, it's worth it! You'll be able to use this information anytime in the future when you're trying to figure out the best time to share your post on Instagram to sure you're getting the engagement you deserve!

Choosing a schedule for posting content

To save time, you should plan your posts for direct publishing. That's good. It means your contents are getting shared consistently. But now, what can be done to make sure it is sharing these posts consistently at the right time?

Iconosquare's Instagram Scheduler is a quick and effective way to schedule all your content. After you've posted enough, the scheduler will should the best time to post your media with a yellow star.

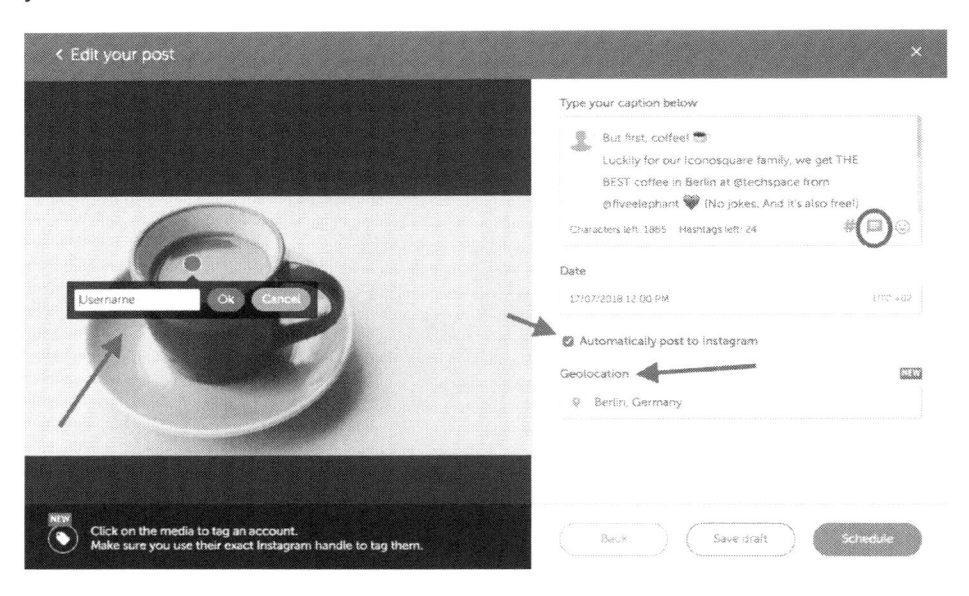

The yellow stars are located at specific slots on the calendar to show some of the best times to publish a post. This is based on your top 5 best times to post (usually determined from engagement) for the previous three months. So, the more the diversified the time you experiment with, the better the accuracy of the suggestions!

With the new Direct Publishing feature of Iconosquare, you can easily schedule your post without the need for push notifications. This means that, even if you're located in Europe and your audience lives in the US, you can still make sure your content is noticed even with the varying time zones. But let's be honest, being asleep while your audience is awake is never a good idea. It is although, a good way to get around the time zone issues.

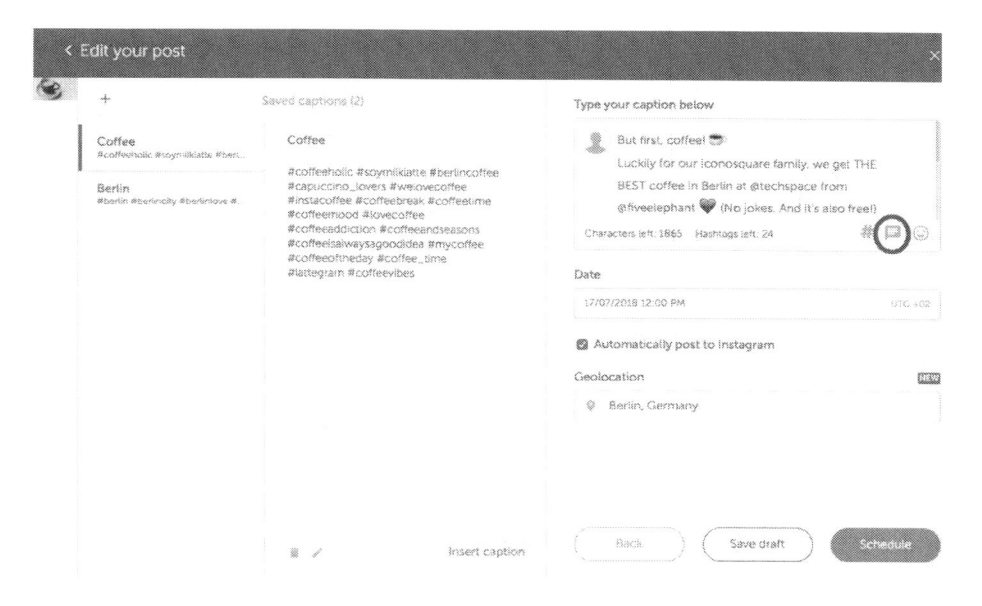

Instagram is one of the best places for businesses to grow online and to also achieve marketing goals. It's not just enough to make a simple post anymore. Being strategic about your posting times is one of the critical factors to success in Instagram especially in 2019.

However, it always takes time.

Don't forget to remind yourself that it's not a sprint, but a marathon. If you're to take data driven decisions, you need to accumulate the data first – and that will take some time.

By scheduling and planning your contents for the best time to post on Instagram, you can boost your engagement, increase your reach, anxiety ultimately gain more customers and followers.

Learning How to Increase Online Sales Exponentially in 2019

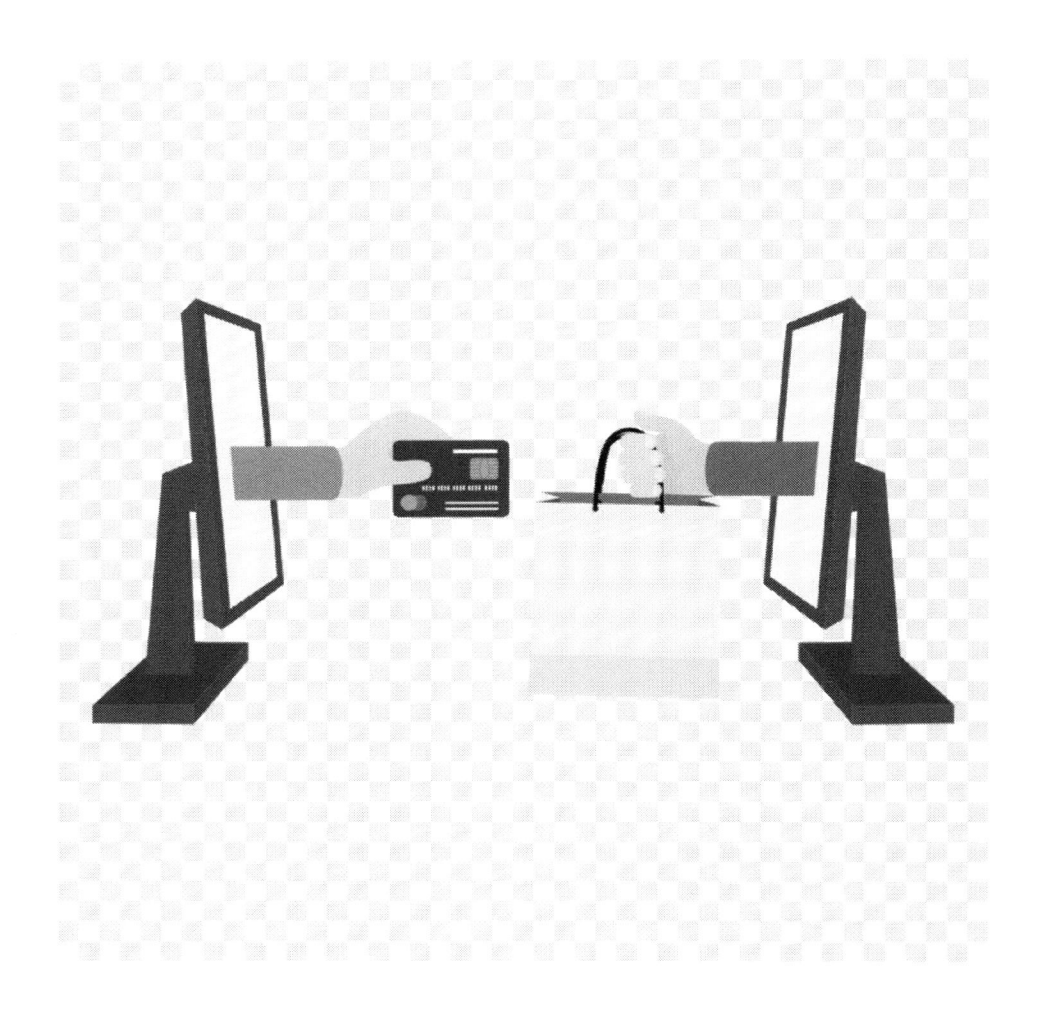

Within the final quarter of 2017, consumers have spent up to $100 billion in the retail e-commerce market. It's no wonder everyone wants to learn about ways to increase online sales.

You want a big slice of that 100 billion dollar pie. E-commerce business, especially in the U.S, is not stagnant. They keep growing every year.

Writing for 360 Commerce about the e-commerce retail growth, Director of Consumers Insights and Research, Stefani Zaroban shows that e-commerce represents at least 49.4 percent of all the retail sales growth in 2017.

There are various customers available to spend their money. So, the billion dollar question is "**how do you increase the online sales of your own business?**"

The Best Ways to Increase Online Sales Fast

I've worked with various companies – SaaS, service business, major retailers, and much more – and I've picked up a few hints on how to increase online sales at a fast pace.

You need an effective strategy that can easily be manipulated over time as your customers and business change.

Growth might sometimes not be consistent. Even though some customers might be buying a lot online, they're not necessarily spending the most on your business. Even some top players in the game like Target sees huge valleys and peaks.

If you want more peaks and fewer valleys, you must pay undivided attention to data and research. You also have to prioritize the needs of all your customers over the needs of your business.

This is the main reason I give away loads of free stuff. It's not because I don't have more important things to do. I give away my contents to spread my brands' awareness, establish my brand, build relationships with potential customers, and also gain their trusts.

In this case, I'm also encouraging reciprocity. If I'm generous enough to offer my knowledge and time, most customers often become generous with their money. This is because they want the same results I got from the strategies I made.

A remarkable contributor to the marketing world, Seth Godin once said "Selling to people that want to hear from you is way more effective than interrupting strangers that don't care.

When you do giveaways, it gives you the chance to connect with people that want to hear your voice.

You can easily use this tactic alongside original content. It is a very effective way to get online sales at a fast rate. I have also compiled various techniques that you can also try.

Reap Trust

If you think that confidence does not matter in relationships, check out the number of companies that experienced huge financial changes just because they had a data breach. An average data breach costs about up to $3.6 million.

Michele Drolet, a CSO contributor, notes that "Breaching must eventually happen, but the various ways you use to mitigate them have a real influence on the bottom line." If you can rebuild your trust after it was broken, you won't experience the same financial loss ever again.

This also goes for any form of breach of trust. For example, if you've broken a promise to your customers, failed to provide credible contents, or provide false information, you lose confidence.

How can TRUST be built? There are a few natural practices to follow.

- Don't make any promise you can't keep. Always keep your word.
- Be transparent: Make sure you continuously provide Insights into your company's workings
- Respond to customers as soon as possible: Always answer customer support questions and help requests.
- Admit mistakes: Everyone makes mistakes, therefore when you do, don't try to covet them up. Instead, provide different ways to fix them.
- Provide case studies: Flaunt the great things you've achieved.
- Cite sources to content. Give credit to others when it's due.

Put all your energy on these practices to ensure an intimate connection between your customers and your brand. You might see an increase in your revenue as a result.

Incorporate product videos

Product photos can be awesome, especially if professionals make them. However, product photos can easily drive customers even to invest more merchandise to the virtual baskets.

An important case study revealed that incorporating product videos can improve the probability of purchase by 144 percent. Stacksandstacks.com also revealed that it's close to a 10-to-1 ROI.

However, it is not necessary to create a video for every product that you sell. You need to focus on one or two bestsellers.

You can even create an explainer, testimonial video, how-to, or demo depending on whether you're a service or product oriented business.

You shouldn't confine your videos to YouTube and your website alone according to Switch Video

Incorporating some important videos in emails has driven click-through rates up to 300 percent. Also, up to 70 percent of marketers that responded to a survey choose video as the most critical factor at rerouted to increased conversions.

You don't need high-grade world-class pieces of equipment to make your video. You can easily create a product video with nothing more than a white sheet backdrop and the camera of your smartphone.

Also, if you want better quality and sound, we recommend you look for a local studio where you can record. You can also find various video editors on freelancer sites like Fiverr who can do a perfect job at a low price.

Focus on your target audience

Finding out the different ways to make more sales online requires an in-depth understanding of the wants and needs of your target market.

Do you have a buyer persona yet? If not, this is the best time to start. A buyer persona gives you an insight into your target customers based on the demographics, dislikes, likes, income, and other personal details.

PERSONA PROFILE

STEVE, 47

Who is he?
- CEO of large financial company worth € 85 million.
- Has been in this role for ten years.
- He is an innovator and isn't afraid to take risks.
- He likes to communicate via email or face-to-face. He is on LinkedIn and Twitter.
- He reads financial and economic publications and attends financial conferences.

BRIGHTSPARK

How he finds us
- He was referred onto by someone he trusts.
- He comes to the website at the beginning of his buying journey.
- He isn't interested in using the information on the site beyond research.

What he wants to know
- Latest projects
- Expertise
- Testimonials
- Awards
- He is looking for a partner-led approach

Why he buys from us?
Price and Expertise

Pain points
- The size of the service team is very important to him.
- There are five other people involved in the buying decision.
- He wants a competitive price with strong experience.

What he doesn't want
- He doesn't want to pay large fees. Value for money is important.

SERVICE TEAMS

Source: Artmarketing

The more the information you include in a buyers persona, the better it becomes. This is because it allows you to target your audience accurately easily. For example, if your target customers include a single mother with one to three children, you can quickly speak with her directly through advertising and marketing.

The content starts to feel more personal.

For instance, let's say you're selling cooking materials. A single mother might be trouble with pain points in her kitchen, such as lack of storage room. If you have combination tools that take less space or smaller tools built for a smaller kitchen, you can readily market to that buyer persona.

Deploy live chat

Live chat gives customers an avenue to converse directly with a chatbot or yourself. Either way, they'll be able to ask essential questions about your services or products and be able to get answers in real time.

Live chat boxes usually look like the old messenger interface. They provide back and forth conversations, usually between consumers and brands rather than friends.

The fastest way to help your customers

Live chat is the best in the field when it comes to customer preference. A survey made by J.D Power revealed that most consumers prefer to live chats Ober social media conversations and emails.

According to another study made by FurstPerson, up to 80 percent of customers refuse to buy any products from a particular brand or company, if they don't have a live chat.

Try to provide live chats with trained and qualified personnel behind tell screens, and your business will be able to nurture customers through an intimate conversation. Every interaction will become an opportunity to convert the customer.

Improve your website's user experience

Various things can influence the multiple ways by which a potential customer navigates and understands your site. Some of the aspects include mobile responsiveness, form design, and page layout.

If you can't afford a professional UX developer, you can still improve the user experience of your website on your own.

You can start this by running scroll maps and heat maps through Crazy Egg. This will help to identify the best part of your website that people mostly engage in.

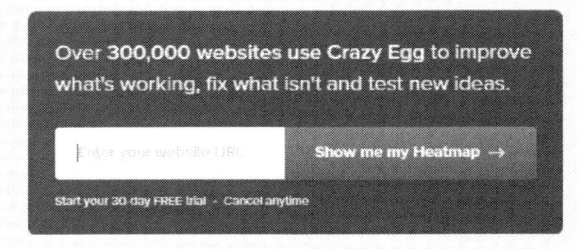

After this, you can easily make decisions about content length, call-to-action placement, navigation placement, and sidebar inclusion, among other things. After you have understood how most people interact and interpret your contents, you can easily make more informed decisions.

Start using Crazy Egg tools!

Remove friction-creating elements on checkout pages

After a customer has gotten to the checkout page, you don't want him to be disturbed. If a customer gets irritated, confused, or distracted, you might lose a sale!

For example, some websites force visitors to create an account before they can purchase any product. This is a bad idea for an e-commerce store, and it might lead to cart abandonment.

While writing for Shopify, Paul Boag said:

"Users didn't come to your site to create an account. They came to buy something."

He then suggested picking a more convenient time to suggest creating an account, using a module as an example.

Wait till the end of the sale, and then allow the customer to create an account.

Elements of friction can include sidebars, extraneous calls to action, and navigation bars.

If your website requires many form fields, your customers might look away simply because they don't have the time to fill all of the templates. Research by Baymard Institute shows that the average form field total for most checkout pages is 4.88 which is twice more than needed.

Author Christian Holst says, "A formally optimized checkout flow should be as short as 7 form fields." Try to eliminate some fields from your checkout form.

Also, streamline your checkout page to reduce distraction and friction. If the pages are intact without an element, remove it so the consumers can stay focused on buying whatever they want.

Offer a guarantee

Satisfaction guaranteed — this is not just a power ballad. It gives various online businesses a chance to help generate more sales.

A famous online retailer known as Land's End uses its satisfaction guarantee as one of its core values. This is how vital the satisfaction guarantee is to the ways business is done.

There's an actual reason for this.

The moment you guarantee your product or service, you have easily eliminated some part of the risk involved in purchasing the item. Your customer won't need to worry about common objections like whether they'll like the product or not, or if it'll hold up.

It still goes farther than this. A guarantee will send an important message that shows you stand behind your product or service. You're willing and able to guarantee it because of its efficacy.

Also, most consumers do not return products even if they don't like it. It takes a lot of effort and tike to box up a product, arrange for the return, buy a shipping label, and also check for the chargeback.

Even if the product is return, you have created some form of goodwill. Besides, up to 70 percent of consumers will not buy a product without looking at the returns policy. With a guarantee, you can easily generate an immediate trust.

The video below shows some useful insider tips that will allow you to offer a money-back guarantee with having to process multiple returns.

Nurture your email list with unique content

Sometimes, marketers usually bombard their emails with advertising type contents, information about upcoming sales, and links to posts. That is not completely bad, but be sure to add unique content and value your mail to increase your marketing strategy.

I received a marketing email from The Mission a while ago. It shows an entire section with contents that customers might find valuable.

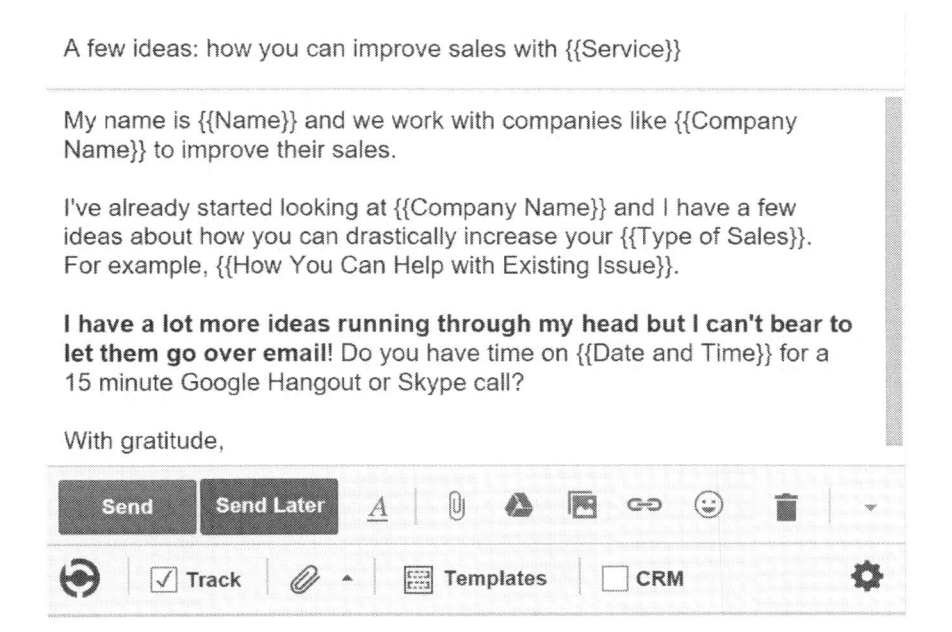

> A few ideas: how you can improve sales with {{Service}}
>
> My name is {{Name}} and we work with companies like {{Company Name}} to improve their sales.
>
> I've already started looking at {{Company Name}} and I have a few ideas about how you can drastically increase your {{Type of Sales}}. For example, {{How You Can Help with Existing Issue}}.
>
> **I have a lot more ideas running through my head but I can't bear to let them go over email!** Do you have time on {{Date and Time}} for a 15 minute Google Hangout or Skype call?
>
> With gratitude,

Instead your usual regurgitating old content, you can try writing unique content for your email selecting campaign. You can also mix things up, but if you regularly share things that are meant for your subscribers only, you can easily drive up sales.

Providing values through your email newsletter does not necessarily mean educational contents. Recent research has shown that up to 23 percent of consumers mostly subscribe to newsletters because of deals.

Don't be stingy with free trials, coupon codes, and discounts. Even if you're offering it once a month, it'll still increase your sales.

Try Crazy Egg Testing Tools to Increase Your Online Sales

Unfortunately, learning about how to increase online sales cannot be done overnight. Although, you can easily hasten the process with some insider information. You also need to look at the long-haul view. If you collect and curate data, it'll be easy to make better decisions for your future.

Crazy Egg allows you to easily analyze many parts of your websites, including heat maps(this will enable you to know where a customer clicked on a link or where he/she stopped scrolling), and UX.

This information will help you to deduce the technicality behind specific visitor behaviors. If most of the users scroll down half the page only, they might be bored with the content, or they might prefer shorter content.

After you've come into conclusion about the users' behavior, conduct an A/B test. Create two identical versions of a landing page, then change just one event. This could be the content or the positioning of the CTA.

After you're done with the A/B test, set up another experiment. Since you're testing a variable at a time, you can easily perfect all aspects of the page.

Respond to your followers on all channels

Engagement is arguably the most important metric to track in online marketing. Your engagement can be defined as the number of interactions you get from your followers, fans, and subscribers.

These are some examples of engagement:

- Responses to social media posts
- Facebook likes
- Email replies
- Retweets
- Answers to polls and surveys
- Blog comments

You can easily track your engagement on social media channels. For example, Facebook Insights allows you to track engagement by post.

Your engagement with others is just as important as your followers' engagement with you. How many times have you stopped to comment on blogs that are leading sources of information in your industry? When people leave comments on your posts, do you reply?

A simple reply like "Thanks, I'm happy you enjoyed it," to a comment on your latest blog posts can spawn conversions. People will welcome the fact that you appreciate them, and they will eventually become fans. These people might subsequently become regular customers.

Jon Suarez-Davis wrote in Adweek, referring to a Salesforce report:

"Up to 80npercent of users explained that the user experience of a company is as important as the product and service they're delivering. If you're able to portray a positive user experience, your online sales will be boosted.

Conclusion

Finding out the best ways to increase online sales is simply determined by getting to know your audience and getting closer to them. If your product or service is top notch, and you provide the best customer service, your sales will increase.

I have compiled several important techniques that can help you grow your sales.

- Use live chats, offer a guarantee, create and post product videos, and make sure the user experience of your website is as frictionless and smooth as possible.
- Providing unique incentives will also help to nurture your email list. Use pop-ups to see how they'll impact the level of your conversation, and make sure you respond to your followers anytime they reach out to you.
- And more importantly, collect and analyze all data available at your disposal.
- Create scroll maps, confetti maps, and heat maps with Crazy Egg. Learn the pattern of behavior of website visitors on your site to know where to put important information like calla to action.

After you've compiled the data and run your tests, make correct changes with what you've learned. After this, create two landing pages and A/B test all their elements one at a time. Don't forget that this test only works if you have data that will back up your previous decisions.

If you're consistent without these techniques, your sales will increase.

21 Facts About Successful Online Businesses That Was Kept A Secret

You'll find various misconceptions on how to run a successful online business nowadays on the Internet. Sometimes, even the most experienced business owners often underestimate the energy, skill, and time it takes to succeed at a business online.

This chapter will look at the various important facts that differentiate the successful online business from the rest. If you're looking to build your very own online empire, pay attention!

1. They grow fast
Although it's rare for an online business to grow overnight, it also rarer for it to take more than a few years. This is usually true in most competitive niches. If you haven't grown after a year or two, there's no better time to reevaluate your business plan.

An important rule of thumb: if your colleagues or trusted advisors are telling you its time to give up, do yourself a favor – consider and listen to them. Sometimes, you can't keep track of everything.

2. They focus on the big picture

Having an online business is not for everyone. If you are the type that focuses more on researching details instead of making plans, setting goals, looking for trends, etc., you are probably not the best candidate for an online business.

3. They differentiate themselves

The e-commerce market is gigantic. Some has estimated that it's a trillion dollar market spread within 12 million online stores. Successful business owners know how crucial it is to differentiate themselves from others so they can easily claim their piece of the pie.

4. They know when to give up

I'm sure you know quite a few "never give up" quotes here and there, but that's not the case here. Business owners should know when to cut their losses absolutely, and generally give you on something or someone. It could be a person, a strategy, or technique entire business venture.

5. They understand the value of great content

Content marketing has now become very important especially when it comes to online business. If you're not producing a stream of valuable, relevant content, there's no way of being successful. If you are still not sure on the best way to begin, read the earlier chapters again.

6. Social media is their weapon

There's no possible way to run an online business with social media accounts. About two years ago, Shareholic shared that at least a third of their referral traffic comes from social media. This number should be incredibly higher today. If you're not using your arsenal of social media accounts to reach new customers to connect with the new ones, you don't have a chance.

7. They go all in

People usually think they can build their online empire with just their time. They put most of their effort and time on other jobs, then fiddle with their business when they like. You can't build a successful online business this way. If you keep treating it like a hobby, it won't be more than that. Make your online business your priority and give it the attention it deserves like a real business.

8. They listen to their customers

Never undermine the value your customers bring to the development and growth of your online business. The founder of Fresh-tops, a highly successful clothing company Nelly Chunky confirmed that customer suggestions gave her the Kickstart she needed for her business to boom. She said "we relied on email suggestions and requests from our social media fans to decide on how to move forward and the items to add to our line, and it worked magically

9. They grow their list from day one

When it comes to most businesses, email marketing is very important. But with online business, it is vital. Qualitative research has shown that email marketing leads to engagement, increased click-through sales, and most importantly sales. Most researchers have suggested that the email provides a higher ROI than most marketing channels. Make sure you build your list from day one to experience the benefits for your business.

10. They pursue their passion

Having an online business can be hard, which is why it is very crucial to be passionate about your business. Ask yourself, can I keep doing this business for the next 5-10 years? If your answer is negative, I believe you should move to another direction and chose something you care about.

11. They know the value they produce, and they charge appropriately

There's no way you'll be able to compete on a long run I'd you keep undervaluing your products or services. It might be tempting to reduce the competition to make a name for yourself, and it's usually beeper to set a price that will be sustainable for your business for the nearest future.

12. They invest heavily in SEO

According to research made by Ascend2, more than 80 percent of marketers believes SEO is getting more effective. Getting a higher ranking in search engines is quite essential for an online business, as it will be your most significant source of traffic. Check out the beginners guide on SEO if you need some help optimizing your site.

13. They solve a real problem

Finding a real need in your particular niche is vital for all types of businesses. What issue or problem can your product or service solve? Does your service or product solve one specific problem? If not, what are the things you can do to solve the problem?

14. They take action before everything's perfect

The creator of GameKlip, Ryan French has excellent advice for business owners: make sure you don't want until things are perfect before you get moving. He wrote "Don't feel like everything has to be in order, or you need to know everything before you start. I didn't know anything about running a business, no idea on how things are manufactured, and how packages are shipped overseas. At this moment, I've shipped thousands of units to up to 80 countries worldwide. It won't be easy, you might even feel like giving up sometimes, but it'll be worth it."

15. They know that passive income is not passive

Most people think that running an online business will give them the time to work short hours while sipping exotic drinks on the beach. Although, it does give you improved flexibility than a regular job, "passive income" is quite a misnomer. Most online business requires the owner to manage and oversee some critical tasks, even if most of the business is highly automated and does not need hands-on involvement. This admittedly won't allow you to lie on the beach and sip margarita all day.

16. They stop looking for the golden goose

There's no easy way out when it comes to building a successful business. Although, many business owners have wasted a ton of time and resources looking for a unique tactic that will make them successful immediately. The truth is, if there were a shortcut, it'd be hard work and persistence. Don't waste your time looking for the magical thing, cool down, and enjoy the process of hard work and tenacity needed to run your business.

17. They outsource. Sometimes, A LOT

A prominent advertising tycoon once said, "Hire people that are better than you, then leave them to get on with the job." This also goes for outsourcing, if you want to be competitive, outsource everything that 1) you don't enjoy doing 2) doesn't come naturally to you. This will give you ample time to place your focus on what you love, which is very important to sustainable growth.

18. They have an actual plan (a written one)

People often have this misconception that online business is to get people to find your website, buy your products and make lots of money. This is entirely untrue for most successful companies, and it's not right for online businesses! A successful online business requires you to have a solid business plan and a documented marketing strategy.

19. They don't let failure beat them up

Just like any other business, failure is part of the journey. Your next step after you've failed is crucial. Content marketing failing? Focus on your in-depth content. Is your SEO not driving traffic? Find different keywords. Carefully study your competitions and find out the things you can emulate.

20. They utilize excellent tools to save time and money

It is almost impossible to find a successful online business that doesn't use at least five amazing tools for their business. I'll argue these fantastic tools are quite crucial for a successful online business. From online invoicing tools to social media management tools, to communication tools, these are essential tools to help save time and money, and also optimize your productivity.

21. They're dominating their niche

If you're taking anything from this post, make sure it's that you don't have to have to worry about competing with the big guns. You should instead, focus your energy on the subset of your industry. Also, do whatever you can to dominate the area. For example, one of my first niches was a Christmas tree storage.

Instead of taking on all the holiday décor industry, we focused on building our reputation when it comes to offering the best storage at the best prices. We quickly developed a 7-figure business with the strategy, something that couldn't have happened if we were going after the big guys.

Influencer Marketing: Best Trends from 2018 And What To Look Forward To In 2019

As we are in the earliest stages of 2019, it the best time to evaluate the common business strategies while planning for the months ahead. As a content writer focused on the marketing niche, I have made some observations on shifts on the industry that could change the current eat you plain your influencer campaign. Also, I have some predictions about the trends to look forward to this year.

It's harder than ever to get seen

As it was predicted last year, algorithms keep evolving on most social media platforms, especially Instagram and Facebook. Reaching a significant target audience is becoming more difficult with all the automated content flagging, ad restrictions, and feed display changes. These are all new modern changes that happened to social media like Instagram with last year. Relatable and authentic contents are now th3 best chance of reaching the right people through organic shares while improving real brand-consumer connections.

Instagram Stories are a hot commodity

The meteoric rise of Instagram Stories started last year, and this gives influencers and brands to provide intimate behind the scenes access. The feature has also improved the audience interactivity with the Swipe-up, Ask Me, and Polls features. With at least 400 million Instagram active users viewing stories all day, it is now becoming one of the best platforms for positive, informal brand conversations.

Engagement rates are the real metric

The number of audiences that responds to an influencer's content is now more imperative than the total number of followers that an influencer has. Brands usually overlook Nano-influencers and micro-influencers (loosely defined as those with less than 1,000 followers and those with less than 50,000 followers). But researchers have found that what they lack in numbers, and they make up for in engagement and loyalty. The direct personal connection they have built with their audiences can be the key to a successful campaign when it comes to ROI and reach.

Agencies can pinch-hit when scale is needed

As regular brands outsource influencer programs, larger business handles influencer programs in-house while relying on various agencies for campaigns. Agencies and brands can work behind each other.

My Predictions

Brands need more transparency from influencers

After the recent exposure of fake followers, brands are now on high alert for frauds and are looking for more insights on those they're working with. Brands can take steps, like weeding out artificially boosted accounts, evaluating the engagement of the influencer to his follow ratio or growth over time or partner with a full-service agent to differentiate compatible influencers from bad ones.

Facebook Live is the new standard for Quality, Value, and Confidence

Within the early weeks of 2018, up to 2 billion people had watched different Facebook Live broadcasts. Some companies use influencer broadcasts with millions of views and six-figure shares. For evoking videos, concentrate on the live audience Q&A and engaging host, also include links with discount codes. Also, Facebook keeps adding various features to make live streaming compelling. Hence brands and companies should start taking notes.

This platform trend is OK to ignore (for now).

Although everybody thinks and hopes Instagram stories will continue to be a hit in 2019, nobody is placing their hopes on IGTV. Instagram's version of a video hub hasn't been working. Its vertical video format is also making it impossible for brands to repurpose contents. We'll keep a close eye, but for now, we're not recommending it.

Agencies will provide influencer education as a service

Expert education has become one of the growing needs for brands that are looking to manage their very own influencer marketing programs. Training sessions and agency workshops for legal marketing stakeholders are also required as the team needs to learn how to avoid disclosure or copyright issues while managing, activating, and recruiting influencers at scale.

The Final Word

If you haven't tried influencer marketing before, now is a perfect time to start. A recent study has shown that match businesses will guarantee you up to 500% for every penny spent on influencer marketing. Also, McKinsey research has shown that induced customer-to-customer word of mouth produces at least twice the sales of the genetic paid advertising in various categories including mobile phones and skincare.

Whether you manage your influencer efforts in-house or you work with an agency, this is the best time to reminisce on 2018 and ask yourself important questions like how content creators and their audiences can help move your business goals forward this year.

Top 10 Nuggets to keep in mind

To summarize this book, I will be touching on ten of the most essential tips and processes that are of paramount importance as you start your journey into the world of influencer marketing. Influencer marketing, as earlier reiterated is a thriving industry and there are many success stories as I'm sure you you know already.

It is easy to have a go at influencer marketing and drop out after a series of unfavorable outcomes and I expect some of my readers to fall under this category. Truth is, it isn't for everyone but it can be for you.

Every chapter, sentence, and word have been carefully crafted to help you achieve tour influencing goals, ad to learn how to make the most of social media platforms, especially Instagram. Without further ado, let us jump into my top ten nuggets and refresh you on the required practices and essential tips that will help launch your successful career.

Also, if you have enjoyed the book so far, be sure to drop a nice 5 star review on Amazon to promote this and share with others like you. There's enough space in the sky for every bird on earth.

1. **Knowing Yourself**
In one of the chapters, we discussed the importance of discovering yourself as this directly translates to the niche you will work on. Being a jewelry enthusiast will help you in the fashion niche largely compared to the automotive industry. Your true passion must lie in what you do. I cannot areas this enough.

If you are an introvert, being an Instagram influencer can be a hard ask. Introverts typically want their space and limit their exposure to people. While being an Instagram influencer requires meetings with brands, Skype calls, constantly engaging followers online, and everything an introvert does not like.

The biggest way to combat these personality traits is to ease into the world of influencer marketing. Substitute calls with emails, Skype calls for IMs, and presentations for live speeches. Gradually, I believe you will learn to accommodate your personal downsides to influencer marketing.

Simply jumping onto the influencer bandwagon because of the money will eventually make your business fizzle out. Your interest in a particular niche and the posts you put up will have a different energy about them if you are genuinely passionate about what you posts. This will reflect with the types of brand you collaborate with. So, discover yourself before you sell yourself.

2. **Hashtags Hold All The Power**
Since its inception and recently with the rise of influencer marketing over the past decade, Instagram has become a metric-based platform and one of the biggest ways to up your engagement rate is hashtags. Hashtags are one of the most far-reaching features on the platform and have the capability to expose you to a wider audience with minimal effort. Identifying trending keywords, or creating an engaging one can be the key to boosting your exposure on the platform. Do your research with the aid of Alexa ranking tools as discussed earlier.

3. Think Like A Brand

They say to catch a thief, you have to think like a thief. In your case, think like a brand if you want to capture the attention of brands, and get their sponsorships. The first place to start is: If I was a brand, how would I search for the best influencers in my industry? What are the challenges my company is facing? And how do I filter my search to differentiate the engaging influencers from generic influencers? These are the questions you need to ask nd make sure to pass the criteria you set for yourself. This will qualify you as a top rated regardless of your follower count.

4. Engagement Rates Matter, Not Follower Count

You don't need bazillion followers to excel as an influencer. Gone are the days where a million followers translate to guaranteed engagements. Brands have finally come to realize that the sole metric to judge a successful influencer marketing strategy is the engagement rates and reach. And smaller accounts tend to have that in surplus due to constant interaction with your followers. The point is, your priority should never be about getting as many followed as you can in minimal time. Work on your engagement levels and make your existing audience the priority.

5. Know Your Target Audience and Research Them

A good relationship with your audience is one of the most essential assets to have in your arsenal as an upcoming influencer. And the biggest way to know your target audience is to research them. There are several ways to achieve this including: using Iconosquare tools, asking directly, hosting interactive sessions, quizzes, Q&A, and many other ways. The upside to these seemingly stressful processes is that understanding your followers gives you an inside look at their thought process, the stuff they like, how they like it, and when they like it.

Researching your target audience will have a direct influence on your posting schedule, your affiliation with certain brands, and how you present your content.

6. Insist On Creating Content Together

The creative process when creating posts is a bit of a learning curve as an upcoming influencer. In many cases, all the work is dumped on you as the influencer. It is very important to have creative control when creating posts. You know your audience best, hence, you should not just get the content from your partnering brand and dish it out to your audience.

You should have the majority of creative control because of your relationship with the audience, and the consequences of posting content that does not resonate with your followers will blow back heavily on you in comparison with the brand. Don't ruin your account because of an overbearing brand and their promise of a fat paycheck. There will be many clients and brands who insist on promoting their content in certain ways that do not bode well with your online persona.

Don't be shy to voice your reservations. You are the Instagram expert here. Stamp your authority on the creative process with the end goal of satisfying your followers.

7. Build A Successful Influencer Marketing Strategy

This is essentially the cornerstone of any successfully influencing career. Usually brands deal with this aspect as each business has its own marketing strategy which they want you to incorporate. Depending on their goals, brands can have different approaches to the market. Personally, you must have a marketing strategy in place to boost your engagement levels, boost your brand exposure, and just incase your affiliate brand does not have one.

There are a variety of tools that deal with the various parts of an influencer marketing strategy. Researching your target audience, researching keywords, reaching out to brands, researching the most prominent hashtags, and researching rankings are all components of a influencer marketing strategy. A combination of Alexa, Iconosquare, Crazy Eggs, and Google analytics tools are available to make this process easier so be sure to whip out the computer savvy nature to get the best of these mostly-free tools.

They will play a crucial role in monitoring and tracking progress, and promoting your content as needed.

8. Remember that Influencer Marketing Is Not Just Another Online Business

If you are looking to sip margaritas and post content once a week in hopes of earning thousands of dollars, then I am here to burst your bubble. Influencer marketing is a real business that requires real structure, hard work, lots of emails, networking, events, and everything you can think of in the corporate world. While it can start out as a side business, if done right, it can overtake your major income in less than a year. This is a fact that I've seen happen many times.

This book is designed to provide you with all the information you need to be a success story. Another Logan Paul. Another Ravie Loso. Another moneymaker. The bigger the effort, the bigger the reward. It's that simple. Everything has been set up to see you succeed.

There are many examples of influencers that started in 2018 and are now household names in their niche. Every business makes use of social media in one form or the other. By tapping into this market, you have the potential to be a leading member in your industry very soon.

But only if you put in the work. In the last two chapter of the book, we discussed 21 tips needed to successfully run an online business. Trust is a big item on that list. Once your followers trust you, there are no limits to what you can achieve. Honesty , trust, and a true willingness to help swell your clients brand are the hallmarks of a great influencer. Strive to be those three and you already have a good headscarf on the competition.

9. It's Okay To Copy The Competition

Replicating a winning formula is just smart business. When you identify bigwigs in the industry that are doing exceptionally well, it is imperative that you network with such names to learn the ropes and adopt practices that you like. Replicating a working formula is basic human nature so do not be shy when researching your competition. You can even partner with them to boost your profile on different social media platforms.

Share4Share is a good way to achieve this. Joining Instagram groups also works well when trying to boost your brand. By working with other influencers, you can integrate well with the general audience and pull your own crowd.

Identify their winning formula, spice it up, improve on it, and followers will start flooding your timeline. That is all there is to it.

10. Instagram Captions Are Engagement Magnets
What draws a follower to your post is the caption and content. But caption first. Instagram Captions perform an incredible job of eliciting the right response from readers and potential followers. By mixing s catchy caption with keyword-rich hashtags, you have an undefeated combination that work 90% of the time. Instagram captions should always be witty and caption without losing the message.

They especially come in handy when trying to engage your followers. Exercises like "Best captions wins blah blah" are a great way to bring out the creative side in your followers.

Spoiler alert: If you're known for your dope captions, followers will be inclined to visit your profile regularly to "borrow" your captions for their pictures. This will automatically make you a fan favorite.

Instagram works best through word of mouth nd referral and you can be sure to get that in abundance with a captivating caption.

I believe theses top ten nuggets have refreshed and added to your knowledge on how to become a successful Instagram influencer and how to run an online business on social media platforms. With the right attitude, and by constantly reading this book, you are guaranteed to boost your brand exposure and have a successful influencer marketing career.

Printed in Great Britain
by Amazon